CHESAPEAKE SPRING

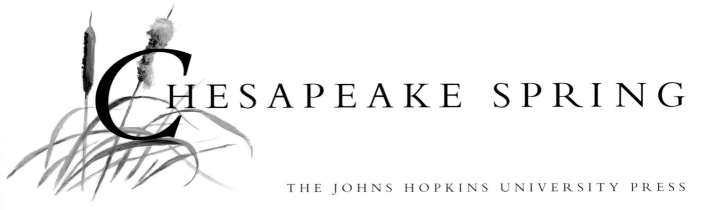

CHESAPEAKE SPRING

THE JOHNS HOPKINS UNIVERSITY PRESS

Baltimore and London

JOHN W. TAYLOR

To all those who are striving
to bridge the gap that
tragically separates human beings
from their fellow creatures.

A Robert G. Merrick Edition

9 8 7 6 5 4 3 2 1

The Johns Hopkins University Press
2715 North Charles Strees
Baltimore, Maryland 21218-4363
The Johns Hopkins Press Ltd., London

A catalog record for this book is available
from the British Library.

Designed by Anita Walker Scott.

Composed by A. W. Bennett, Inc., of Hartland,
Vermont in Adobe Bembo text and display.

Printed on acid-free paper and bound by
C & C Offset Printing Co. Ltd. in Hong Kong.

Library of Congress Cataloging-in-Publication Data

Taylor, John W. (John William), 1931–
Chesapeake spring / John W. Taylor.
—A Robert G. Merrick ed.
p.   cm.
ISBN 0-8018-5765-1 (alk. paper)
    1. Natural history—Chesapeake Bay (Md. and Va.)
2. Spring—Chesapeake Bay (Md. and Va.)   I. Title.
QH104.5.C45T39   1998
508.3163'47—dc21   97-24300   CIP

CONTENTS

PREFACE & ACKNOWLEDGMENTS

This book is not a literal relating of one particular spring on the Chesapeake. Journal selections from many years form a composite, bound together by the common threads of time and place and with a degree of artistic license.

The body of the text is adapted from field journals kept for more than twenty-five years. I have chosen only entries that best tell the story of spring on the Chesapeake. It was my custom to take notes in the field then rewrite them later the same day, elaborating from memory and adding details from research.

The journals that resulted were intended to preserve any scientific value from the day's observations and to somehow rescue fragments of my emotional response to close contact with the natural world. There was at first no anticipation of, nor any consideration given to, potential readers. As I revised for publication, my perception of a reader's response sometimes changed both the tone and the content of the entry. In other instances the selections are taken almost verbatim.

For those interested, the scientific names of the animals and plants mentioned are given in an appendix at the back of the book. A listing of place names and their general locations is also provided.

All of the artwork was done expressly for the book and relates closely to the text.

Without the patient indulgence of Jack Goellner, Director Emeritus of the Johns Hopkins University Press, this book would never have been completed. It was he who, once the seed had been planted, believed it viable and provided the soil, a fertile blend of encouragement, forebearance, and criticism, in which it could grow. His influence is felt on every page.

I have benefited from the kindness and expertise of many naturalists and biologists, both professional and self-taught. Personnel from three government agencies, the Maryland Department of Natural Resources, the Anne Arundel Department of Parks and Recreation, and the Maryland National–Capitol Park and Planning Commission, have been especially cooperative. At the risk of leaving out deserving others, I would single out Gene Deems, Arnold Norden, Lorrie Byron, and Jim Mowrer from the state agency, and Greg Kearns and Jeff Mauck from the county departments. I am grateful to Harry Armistead, Bill Miles, and Pam and Wade Stephen, for ferrying me out to islands in the Bay and for sharing with me their experience in the ways of wild things. I received valuable advice and criticism from Jim Hoverman and John Dougherty, who read the manuscript in various stages of its completion. I want to acknowledge the invaluable assistance of Margot Parker, librarian at the Anne Arundel Community College. And finally, it was the skilled hand of manuscript editor Celestia Ward that welded together such a mosaic into a readable whole.

INTRODUCTION

This book is about convergence, about the coming together of a particular time and a special place.

The time is spring, that segment in the earth's orbit in which the natural world awakens, a season of dramatic change and spectacular migrations, of growth and flowering, of hatching and birthing.

The place is the Chesapeake Bay, an especially favored body of water known for its beauty and its bounty. An estuarial mix of salt and fresh water, it supports a wealth of marine life. Marvelous creatures have their being in its depths and derive their sustenance from its waters and shores. Its pine-rimmed marshes and remote islands nurture a unique and abundant flora and fauna. Even where its shores are intensely developed, there persists a surprisingly varied community of wild creatures.

To the miracle of spring, the Chesapeake lends a special amalgam of climatic, geographic, and natural features. The relationships between land and water, between the winds and tides and currents, have a direct bearing on the cyclic rhythms of nature. All contribute to the character of the Bay, to its moods—the dead calms, the luminous gray fogs, the lusty nor'easters. There are other estuaries, other broad marshes and island vistas, but only here have the forces of nature joined in such a unique commingling.

Superimposed on the geologic and geographic features of the bayscape and on the gradual change of the seasons are sudden, irregular fluctuations in the earth's atmosphere. The Chesapeake is especially susceptible to these influences. Lying midway between the sources of cold polar air and warm tropical masses, the Bay is continually charged with the tensions between these extremes. Often it is the wind, not the calendar, that calls the tune.

This conflict between warm, active southern air and cold, heavy winds from the north stubbornly resists any gentle, regular turn of the seasons. When the Bay area is favored by a strong, southerly flow of air, temperatures may reach 60 degrees in January; wind from a northern quarter can, with no mercy, change April to December. Its lack of allegiance to north or south, hot or cold, make it a place diverse and unpredictable.

So on the Chesapeake there is little consistency in the turn of the seasons. Indeed, one could hold with good cause that there are not four seasons at all in this part of the world, but only two: spring and fall. For one half of the year, the days become progressively longer; during the other half, the amount of daylight lessens. Similarly, with some variation, a graph of average daily temperatures shows a continuing rise for six months, followed by a corresponding decrease, dividing the year equally.

In Chesapeake latitudes, the first day of winter might well count as the first day of spring. Already there are indications of an awakening, a renewal, despite the extreme cold or deep snow that is to come.

Warm days in late December may briefly rouse the first spring peeper or inspire the rollicking cadence of a Carolina wren. Bald eagles show mating behavior around Christmastime and begin nest building in January. Great horned owls keep to the same schedule. Both of these raptors, nesting on the shores of the Bay, are often incubating their eggs while there is still snow on the ground.

It is spring in January when the song sparrow first sputters a hesitant little jingle or when the redwings begin to tune up in the frozen marsh. It is spring in February when the spathes of skunk cabbage emerge through panes of ice, the heat from their expanding leaves melting the snow around them.

It takes but a few mild days to bring out the first flowers on the bitter cress in the fallow fields of the Delmarva Peninsula. The common chickweed, though a troublesome weed to many, offers a welcome bit of color even in January. Both of these plants have come to bloom on New Year's Day in the Baltimore area. The sky-blue petals of a speedwell may unfold coated with January ice. The days become noticeably longer in February. In the lingering twilight, one can hear the musical twittering of the woodcock, performing its sky dance. This mating ritual can occur when the temperature is just above freezing, and nesting may begin by the end of the month in the flood plains along the Chesapeake.

By late February, the male red-wings are in full voice, proclaiming territorial rights even before their mates have returned from the south. Others of their kind are migrating north, straggling flocks winging across the late afternoon skies. These blackbirds, along with the grackles, are perhaps the earliest migrants to appear along the Chesapeake's shores.

February sees yet another rite of spring. Waterfowl begin to show signs of courtship and mating. Among rafting groups of canvasbacks and scaup, one notices various nudgings, bumpings, noddings, and other strange antics, accompanied by assorted coos, grunts, and coughs. Wigeon and teal are more forthright, engaging in rapid chases and flying pursuits. Should there be a warm rain even in February, the earliest of the amphibians begin to stir. Spotted salamanders wander in search of breeding pools, and wood frogs congregate for their brief annual fling.

Before spring officially begins on the calendar, the surge of bird migration is in full swing. Skeins of honking geese enliven the skies, and armadas of tundra swans await the south wind that will take them to the Great Lakes on the first leg of their journey to the Artic Circle. Ospreys return to the Bay area weeks before the spring equinox. According to Maryland tradition, they are expected to show up first on Saint Patrick's Day. But often they are here two weeks sooner, and within days they have begun gathering sticks for nest repair.

So then, by the time of the equinox, when the calendar says spring has arrived, the natural cycle of life has long since begun to turn. With the longer days and the changing angle of the sun, temperatures become more constant, the weather less temperamental. No longer does ice skim the creeks each morning; the Bay waters finally begin to warm.

Water warms much more slowly than the surrounding air and does so in varying degrees depending on depth and salinity. Rising temperatures trigger the migratory instinct in fish, driving them into fresher waters to spawn. As spring progresses, conditions become suitable for a succession of species.

Most years, yellow perch begin to school and move to spawning grounds when the water reaches 45 degrees. White perch like warmer water, so they wait until about two weeks later. It is normally not until April that the alosids—the herring, shad, and alewives—move upstream to spawn. The alewives are first, reaching the heads of the narrowest tributaries by late March if the water has warmed to 50 degrees. Blueback herring spawn from mid-April through late May, tolerating a wider range of temperatures (57–77 degrees). Early April signals the beginning of the shad run (what is left of it these days), which may last through early May, until the water is about 77 degrees. Rockfish also have a lengthy spawning period, lasting from April through May, as long as the water does not warm to more than 70 degrees.

Traditionally, the shad begin to move upstream when the shadbush bursts into flower. The thin, delicate petals, which give this shrub its other name, shadblow, create a welcome contrast in the bare woods. Since there are at least two varieties of shadbush in the Chesapeake region, the period of bloom may last into April's third week. Often commingling with the white of the shadbush is the deep magenta of the redbud, a shrub that may reach treelike proportions along the Chesapeake. But most years, it is the yellow flowers of the spicebush that first star the spring woods.

Just as a Chesapeake spring is like no other, so each Chesapeake spring is itself exceptional. One year the trees may come to leaf in late March; the next, if it remains cold and rainy, may see little green until mid-April. One spring, March may bring the first warbler, a yellow-throated or a pine; another year, we may not hear them until weeks later. But there is one constant you can bet on: tomorrow the sun will rise a minute earlier than it did today.

As spring advances, the changes become less dramatic. When foliage, already green and expanding, grows yet another inch, the transformation is less noticeable than was budding and flowering against the naked woods. Normally, by mid-May the trees are well in leaf and, by month's end, the aspect is one of summer fullness. From then on, it is a process of nature applying the final touches.

This period of merging, of spring turning into summer, is prime growth time for marsh vegetation and for the submerged aquatics that carpet the bottoms of the clearer, less silted corners of the Bay. The widespread horned pondweed form floating beds of rich green. In the fresh marshes, growth is rampant; a shriveled, winter-flattened wetland becomes head-high in but a few weeks. Salt marshes must cope with a tougher environment and so the spartina grasses there develop slower.

June brings to culmination that part of the life cycle that began in March and April. The eagles that courted in December now have young that are ready to fledge. Rockfish fry that came to life in April are now foraging on their own. Seeds have germinated and grown to leaf and blossom, and, in some cases, in turn produced seed.

With the summer solstice, as the earth begins its great orbital heave, the longest day of the year is at hand. The days will become shorter for the next six months, the sun rising progressively later and setting earlier. And though the hottest days of the year are to come, temperatures on the average will decline until the winter solstice.

Taken literally, *solstice* means that the sun stands still. But there is no standing still. The earth keeps turning. The rhythms of life and growth go on. Moon-driven tides will continue to wash upon Chesapeake shores.

CHESAPEAKE SPRING

DECEMBER 26

West River

The sun had the afternoon sky to itself but for a lone swirl of high cloud, pale against deep azure. The river rested unruffled, touched with the same blue. Across its broad reaches, near the far shore, a raft of ducks relaxed, most of them sleeping, heads tucked into back feathers. A closer look revealed a gathering of squat little ruddies, tails cocked skyward. Beyond, gulls loitered on wharf pilings. (Gulls always seem to have plenty of time to stand around, doing nothing.) And half a dozen swans tipped peacefully in the shallows.

A shrill cackling from above shattered the calm. I looked up just as an eagle folded its wings and plummeted earthward. After falling several hundred feet, it threw out its legs and flared up into the path of another eagle. The two tumbled together awkwardly for a moment, then recovered composure as they gained altitude. Tracing slow, lazy circles in the blue, they came together several times, almost brushing wings.

From that height they could look down on all of West River and on their eyrie, an accumulation of sticks and small branches in the highest fork of a white oak. Half of the mass had been dislodged during a recent storm and had fallen into the lower portions of the tree. Repairs will have to be made within the next few weeks, before egg laying begins.

The eagles did not call again, nor show any courtship activity, but that brief bit of interplay marked a turn toward the season of birth and renewal—toward spring. Yet by the calendar it was winter that had just begun.

JANUARY 16

Patuxent River County Park

It was sullen and overcast much of the day, with a chilly wind, but near dusk fiery streaks showed on the horizon and the sun, just before it set, glowed with an intense red-orange. The sky smoldered briefly with this eerie brilliance, which brushed only the treetops.

At that moment, a spring peeper piped from a marshy roadside ditch. One long note, frail and tentative. A pause, and the tiny frog called again. Could it have been roused by this strange and sudden light? Or did it respond to a slight rise in the temperature?

The peeper will certainly fall back into hibernation during the ice, snow, and cold that is to come. And it will be late March or early April before the wetlands ring with their clamorous nuptial rites.

And yet, here in January, sounded the very first voice of spring. It spoke of the return of life, of the force and promise that pulses even within the merest bits of life.

JANUARY 17

Beverly Beach County Park

For two days south winds had generated a strong flow of warm air. With the balmy winds came vaporous mists, silvering the landscape.

Moisture had condensed on every surface. Every twig, each blade of grass, even the pine needles glistened with tiny droplets of water. First light was a pallid suffusion on the horizon.

From this murk emanated a serene, melodious murmur, barely audible. The warmth had stirred a troupe of wintering robins to song, their voices breathing an inexpressible sweetness and clarity. Tinged with melancholy, the subdued strains radiated a sense of joy, of well-being.

The singing birds were pausing from their primary concern of the season: finding enough to eat. They had flocked to a grove of holly trees, where they hovered and fluttered to reach the bright red berries. Some of them dropped to the ground and scratched among the leaves; others bathed in a marshy streamlet.

But the singing was not casual or incidental. At intervals, each flew in turn to the topmost branches of an oak, where, relaxed and unhurried, it joined others in this quiet, deliberate caroling. There seemed to be a communion, a comradeship among them. In contrast to this song was the staccato chatter they used to keep in touch and the occasional harsh alarm calls.

These were not new arrivals,

3

migrants returned early from the South; rather, they were wintering robins, keeping to the woodlots, feeding on fruits and berries, and roaming about in flocks. They will come to lawns and backyards when it warms enough for earthworms to emerge.

FEBRUARY 4

Sellman Creek

A sliver of light near the horizon, crisply delineated by the dark opaque sky above it, defined the sunset. Under the layer of low cloud, a dim half-light lingered over the marshes and the frozen, snow-covered river. The woods beyond were nearly lost in the dusk.

Tidal action had opened the ice along the shoreline, the water there reflecting the color of the sky. But most of the creek was still frozen; only a patch of open water glinted in the distance. From that direction, I could hear the contented gabble of feeding swans interspersed with the occasional whistle of a wigeon. A rolling trill overhead, with the tone and quality of a shorebird, was probably the call of a wintering dunlin.

Another sound, from across the far shore, I could not identify: a mysterious yelp, followed by a raucous

squalling. Silence. Then again it came, spine-tingling, indescribably wild. But I could see nothing in the dimness that lay beyond the ice-covered creek.

Moments later, across the frozen whiteness scampered a red fox. Near the far shore but in plain sight it hurried, crossing a broad cove. It trotted nimbly over the slippery surface, a sensuous joy in its motion, in the deli-

cate contact it made with the earth and in the way its tail, held high, flowed behind.

It paused in the very center of the cove and looked back from where it had come. Continuing through a bit of marsh to the wooded shore, it seemed to relax, slowing its pace and poking about the undergrowth. It stopped to urinate twice, once on the ice and again after climbing the bank. The fox did not lift a leg while doing so; rather, it assumed a squatting position, lowering its hindquarters and remaining on four legs. Was this the vixen, marking her territory or leaving a trail her mate could follow? And was that weird, shrieking sound a pair of mating foxes? The young are conceived in January and February in these parts, with a gestation period of about fifty days.

Returning along the trail well after dark, I heard a flurry of terrier-like yapping, more shrill than a dog's, from the woods where the fox had crossed the cove. For the foxes, it was spring in snowy February.

Pennington Pond

Temperatures have been seasonably cold for the past week. At sunup the thermometer read 26 degrees and a skim of ice had formed on the pond. But in the early sunshine it felt like spring to an irrepressible male redwing. Balancing atop a cattail spike and flaunting his epaulets, three times he delivered the mating, or territorial, song. A bit rusty, perhaps, but each time he gave the full rendition, beginning with that sustained, liquid note that sounds so much like the plop of a stone into water: "konk-a-reeee." Rising above the marsh, he concluded with a harsh chatter, hovered briefly, then sailed—or "kited"—down with that unnatural fluttering motion associated with a full courtship display.

Perhaps taking its cue from the redwing, a Carolina wren offered, just once, its lively yodel. And a chickadee whistled its four-part strain, a call usually not given until spring is well advanced. Even a song sparrow, quiet and docile, contributed a small and half-remembered song.

It was but a brief musical interlude. Cold silence followed as the day grew dark and blustery.

Beverly Beach County Park

After a week of extreme cold, temperatures have moderated, reaching 50 degrees by midafternoon. Again the robins, still in the holly groves, were moved to song, as were the redwings in the marshes. And once more a song sparrow caught the spirit, delivering a hardly recognizable jumble of notes, out of tune and in need of practice.

Offering even more promise for the coming spring were bright bits of blue that magically appeared on a grassy roadside: the diminutive flowers of a speedwell. Barely half an inch wide, each blossom had four petals, which formed an uneven cross and were veined with darker blue. A healthy mass of rounded, hairy leaves had already formed on a tangle of prostrate reddish stems. Unopened budding flowers dangled on the delicate stems.

Could such growth have developed in one or two mild days? Three days ago the earth here was covered with snow, and little of it has melted. More than likely, rosettes had developed earlier, probably during the early fall, and had been awaiting the first warmth of the season.

FEBRUARY 12

Beverly Beach County Park

It grew cold last night, well below freezing, and I had expected the little blue speedwell to be closed or shriveled. But this morning the delicate flowers were still open, made even lovelier by a coating of frosty rime.

FEBRUARY 13

Pennington Pond

In dark swirling drifts, a battalion of large black birds descended into the backyard and settled into the adjacent trees. They swarmed over the lawn and the feeding shelves, their raucous clamor cutting through the afternoon chill. The grackles were back!

The first birds to return from the South are not robins or bluebirds. And not the honking echelons of Canada geese, which signal to many the end of winter. No, they are the common grackles, a noisy, squabbling, ubiquitous species some would call vulgar. They have abominable social habits (they attack and kill smaller birds) and voices like creaking rusty gates.

A noise frightened them and they rose with a rushing roar, blackening the branches where they came to rest. They soon scrambled back to the feeders, but, restless and anxious to be on their way, stayed only a few minutes. Later, near dusk, a wavering skein of them passed overhead, high up and northward bound, their clucking notes muted by the distance.

FEBRUARY 14

West River

Twilight lingers now, the sun setting a full thirty-two minutes later than it did a month ago. And though temperatures have remained below freezing, life on the Bay is responding to the increasing intensity and different angles of light. Birds especially have been physiologically awakened by such stimuli.

Indeed, light is a dominant force in the life of birds. To find enough of it, they fly thousands of miles every year. They welcome it at dawn, and salute the sunset and the moonrise with their song. The changing angle of light seems to be a critical factor in triggering the migratory instinct. And, above all other factors, it is the intensity of light that determines the time for courtship and mating.

At twilight, the lengthening day had stirred the mating instincts of a party of canvasbacks. Though it was quite cold and much of the river here was still iced over, the ducks were bunched in a pool of open water. They appeared to be little more than silhouettes against an orange glow, the dying sun reflecting on the water.

From their midst issued quiet, guttural sounds, mixed with softer cooing. The calls were so faint, and delivered with such little effort, that it seemed as if the birds were merely breathing, or even snoring, rather than vocalizing. Darkening skies lent an aura of mystery to these curious strains. One canvasback drake threw his head back in a typical courtship gesture, but with none of the parrying and pursuing that would come later.

A layer of cloud swallowed the sun, and the ducks quieted as a pair of great horned owls began an antiphonal duet from the wooded slope above. Each called with a distinctive rhythm and pattern. One began with a series of low, grunting notes that increased in volume and tempo before ending in six resonant hoots. Its mate, I suspect the male, responded with five hoots, just as the other was beginning, so that their voices overlapped, blended. The performance continued in the deepening dusk, the female usually initiating the sequence. But once or twice it was the male that called first, the female joining in immediately.

Both were out of sight until one took flight and landed on a ragged pine, its form a dark shape against the reddening sky, ear tufts flopping about as it turned expectantly back toward its mate. I could see him (again, I think it was the male) bow deeply and raise his rump when he called. The answering hoots excited him to lift and shiver his wings. Finally, on ponderous rounded wings, with his short tail fanned wide, he sailed across an open field, settling atop a cedar copse. The night shift had taken over.

West River

The main channel of the Bay remained ice-free, but the smaller tributaries and inlets and nearly half of this estuarine river had frozen over. Wavelike ripples and odd concentric patterns textured the ice. A number of nearly perfect circles appeared white against a darker ground. What formed these sweet and graceful curves? The wind? The tide? Freezing and thawing?

Far across the ice, next to the shoreline a heron crouched, its breast plumes catching the wind. A bit of open water there may have furnished some meager fare for this gaunt, spindly-shanked creature, which looks half-starved even in the best of times. On the ice near the great blue heron rested a pair of black ducks.

In a sliver of open water swam a party of goldeneyes. Hardy ducks, they dived and preened, oblivious to the cold and wind. Nor were they bothered by the eagle standing on the ice only a few yards away, even though it had just hovered briefly over them in an apparent attempt to learn if any of the waterfowl were weak or injured.

Taking to the air again, the eagle crossed the river to a wooded promontory, coming to rest high upon an oak stub. Nearby, the white head of its mate showed just above a mass of sticks, conspicuous among the surrounding bare branches. The larger female rose from the nest, standing upright—an action that brought the male to her side. Together they perched for eight or ten minutes near the nest, so close they appeared to be touching each other. The male seemed to preen the wing feathers of its mate for a few moments, before sailing off along the shoreline. The female followed, the two rising to a considerable height then soaring in great circles over the Bay and the wooded peninsula. Twice they approached each other, brushing wings, but made no further contact.

At close of day, a crimson sunset glowed beyond a cold and snowy landscape. It offered barely enough light to see the male eagle glide to the nest and join his mate. Eagles, which mate for life, apparently roost together in their nest. I thought of them, huddled there throughout the long winter night on that exposed treetop.

Sellman Creek

After a spell of cold and wind, with a snowfall, the weather had turned mild. The warmer air circulating over the snow cover generated a heavy mist, veiling the landscape and blending marsh with woodland, sky with water. The haze thickened as the day ended, the sun a smoky glow at the horizon.

A pall of silence enveloped the land as well; I heard not a single bird in an hour's walk. Then, in the shadowy dusk, the quiet was broken by an abrupt burst of bird chatter. A bevy of white-throated sparrows began to call, anxiously answering one another. The sharp, metallic notes ran together in excited confusion.

Above this babble rose a fragment of whistled song, clear and sweet, yet pensive, wistful. A lone whitethroat had given voice to the spring song. Just once: a sustained whistle, followed by two quavering notes slurring upward on a different pitch. Though not as full in its present delivery as the song would be on the breeding grounds, it breathed the same poignancy there in the misty dusk.

The sudden outbreak of chipping calls, the roosting or "rallying" cere-mony of the whitethroats, can be heard each winter evening just before dark. One learns to expect it when the light has dimmed below a certain intensity. For a small bird, going to bed can be risky business, a matter of life or death. It must find at the same time shelter, warmth, and protection from predators. The whitethroats, in their nervous concern, seemed to seek the comfort of their comrades at this crucial time in their day.

Patuxent River County Park

Only a week ago, eight inches of fresh snow covered the frozen earth. Fresh water ponds and streams had been iced over for more than a month. So, though it had warmed to 55 degrees by late afternoon, it was surprising to hear the steady piping of those tiny, inch-long frogs, the spring peepers. Normally such a chorus would not resound until mid-March or later.

The din rose from a shallow depression filled with rain and melt water. Nearing the pool, I could also hear the croaking of wood frogs, cacophonous and grating but not as shrill or as loud as the calls of the peepers. At close range it sounded much like the soft clucking of contented hens. Breaking the surface all around were bulging eyes and frog snouts. The water swirled with movement, forming spreading circles and ripples. All I could find at first were wood frogs; the peepers were but voices in the bog.

Some frogs floated passively, while others darted away with strong thrusts of long, thin legs. Many embraced in pairs. So intense was the mating urge that I was able to study them from a few feet. Pairs that did move off swam while still clasping. Some lay flat on the bottom, slender and delicately mottled with tawny brown. The yellow line along the sides of the jaw was distinctive. The very large eyes were rimmed with the same golden hue. Less distinguishable under the water were the dark brown cheek patches. From their eyes shone a dim light, primitive, timeless, inscrutable.

It was obvious which were the females. They were either grasped from above or closely attended by one or two smaller males. Females were nearly twice as large as their consorts, and were lighter and more reddish in color. A more prominent striping marked their legs.

The gelatinous egg masses were clumped in one corner of the pool. Beneath the water they looked dull and silvery; in one's hand they were clear as glass. The suspended eggs were dark brown, the size of BBs.

The wood frogs seemed little disturbed as I stood virtually over them. I even managed a few photographs, though the light was fading. But the peepers remained wary, out of sight. They quietened as I stepped toward them, and though I carefully studied every blade of grass, I could not find a one.

Just before it grew too dark, however, I caught the movement of a tiny frog as it climbed onto a sedge leaf. For a moment it was in full view. As I leaned closer it wriggled away beneath the vegetation. But instantly it began to call and, though partially hidden, its swollen throat gleamed like a bubble in the last light of the day. From it issued a proclamation: the earth is alive again.

FEBRUARY 26

Eastern Neck Island

A gray dawn followed two days of fog and rain. But early in the day a steady breeze from the north began to disperse the overcast, driving billows of mist across the water. By late afternoon the wind had strengthened, blowing strong and cold from the northwest. It drove water far into the tawny marshes bordering the island, arching the backs of the grasses, bending them to half their height.

At sundown only a few tatters of cloud remained, framing a fiery orb as it dropped below the horizon. The undersides of the clouds were tinted a rosy orange, the same colors reflecting in the choppy Bay waters that danced before the sun. Puddles of rainwater glowed like patches of sky.

From one of these cornfield rain pools issued a slow creaking trill, much like that made by running a finger along the teeth of a comb. A voice of spring emerged above the whine of a February wind. The warmth of the past few days, along with the heavy rains, had awakened a chorus frog, no bigger than a quarter, from its winter's sleep.

Across the inlet, resting in the shallows, were more than two hundred tundra swans. Their tooting melted into the wind. Dark against the twilit water, many of them slept, their serpentine necks twisted, heads tucked into backs. Such a convocation of swans was yet another sign of the turning season. This particular corner of the Bay has long been one of their staging areas, a gathering place before beginning the long migration to the Arctic Circle. The moment of departure waited upon weather and wind.

MARCH I

Taylor's Island

A cold day, milky pale, the sun was veiled with a featureless tissue of cloud. The marshes here were full of the stir and talk of waterfowl, infused with the feel of spring, gripped with the urgency of life. Courting parties veered and twisted above the grasses, vanishing when they settled into the water and reappearing when the chase resumed.

The cricketlike piping of the green-winged teal drakes betrayed their numbers, hidden beyond the screen of phragmites. Though but a single syllabled monotone, the sound is one of the loveliest bits of natural music we have. So mellifluous, so tonally pure is their fluting, that the blend is magic when flocking birds call in unison.

Bands of these pint-sized ducks lifted from the marshy expanse, in mock or real pursuit—or (so it seemed) merely for the pure joy of flight. After dashing upward they would drop suddenly or turn abruptly, white bellies flickering as they wheeled. One cluster of them cork-screwed downward for several hundred feet, erratic as falling leaves, emerald wing patches glinting. Most were in tightly knit bunches of six or eight, but one gathering, roused by a passing harrier, was massed like thrown confetti.

Gadwall, wigeon, and a contingent of pintail were present, too. Half a dozen yellowlegs fed on a grassy flat, but, out of character, they were quite silent. A faint, grating purr carried in the wind identified a trio of passing dunlin.

Later, I came upon about thirty of these shorebirds resting on a beached log just offshore. Dusky gray at this season, with whitish accents, their curved bills created pleasing silhouettes. Suddenly they leapt to flight. Over the water they showed dark backs then, all at once, light bellies as they twisted in perfect unison. Around they whirled, like shoaling fish, first up the beach, then down. Most of them soon returned to the same log they had just left, but a few settled lightly on the beach. Hardly had they touched the earth, delicate feet hanging tentatively, when they were off again.

South River

Just before nightfall, from very high over the Bay, fell a faint murmuring, barely audible. Tundra swans migrating! Mellowed by the distance, the haunting sound grew louder as the birds came nearer, and became more of a yelping whoop. One could feel the tense excitement in their voices, as if they sensed the import of the moment. It was the first stage of a journey that would eventually take them within the Arctic Circle.

I heard their calling several minutes before I could find them in the darkening sky. In a ragged, wavering *V*, they numbered about 150 fifty birds. Long necks extended, they drove themselves forward with short, steady thrusts, moving only the tips of their wings. At that height, they caught the low sun, which no longer touched the landscape below them.

On a course to the northwest, the swans disappeared into the rosy light at the horizon, their calls trailing after them. I guessed that they would fly most of the night, and, with the south wind behind them, keep a cruising speed of seventy-five miles per hour. I imagined their landfall, a marsh-fringed pond on the Canadian border

remembered by the older birds in the flock.

Later, toward midnight, more swans passed over. Their calls, falling mysteriously from the night sky, indicated two or three large flocks traveling at considerable altitude.

MARCH 13

Turkey Point

Though the morning was cloudless, a heavy ground fog hovered over the Bay, shrouding even the nearest shorelines. The sun, breaking through, tinted wisps of rising vapor and spread saffrons across the sky.

A flicker began its spring song, drumming on a resonant tulip poplar stub that reached above the fog. Responding to the message, another flicker appeared suddenly, lower on the stub. This sent the drummer (a male, showing his moustache) into a frenzied round of courtship display. Calling "wicka, wicka, wicka," he spread his tail wide to show the bright yellow feathers and bowed toward the other, weaving from side to side in a wide arc. After a brief spell of this posturing, he drummed again and spread his golden tail.

Two crows barged in, interrupting this tryst, but the bond had been formed. Later, I noticed the woodpeckers taking turns at digging a nest hole. Showing great interest in this project was a pair of starlings, also in need of a nesting cavity. One starling busied itself investigating every possible nook and cranny, even entering a mailbox to explore the potential there. (The starlings may well appropriate the flickers' excavation as soon as it is finished.) Such nesting instincts were the first indications of the season among the songbirds.

The day passed without a cloud. The temperature reached 70 degrees, rousing the spring peepers to a concert that lasted well into the night. Above their babel, I could hear the calls of old squaws migrating in the darkness.

MARCH 18

Corrotoman River

Earlier, a fabric of mist had hung over the river, draping the wooded rises where oaks budded green amid the wine red of maple flowers. Puffs of fog wreathed about dark pines standing on shore. But by midmorning a bright sun had cleared the air, illuminating with sudden clarity different aspects of the landscape. It cast a pink-ish light on the slopes above the river and on wooded islands rising from the marshes. It shone on the farmlands and fields beyond, as well as on a distant field of yellow mustard. It caught pools of water in the swampy bottom lands.

Overhead a hawk soared, giving the harsh, strident peal of a red-shoulder. Sailing in wide circles, it gained height, calling all the while. Abruptly, with closed wings, it began an accelerating, slanting dive, and just above the trees it passed close to its mate. It descended out of sight, then reappeared, climbing in a steep spiral. Reaching a sufficient height, it dropped once more, picking up momentum, legs dangling loosely and wings partially closed. Throughout its display a strident, almost pained, scream rent the air. In response, the female offered fainter, clucking sounds.

Tiny blue butterflies, spring azures, fluttered along the riverside trail. A pine warbler trilled—all on one pitch, but without a hint of monotony. A steady thrum of blackbird banter filled an alder thicket, their lively chatter mixed with liquid whistles.

Popham Creek

An uneasy quiet brooded over the Bay and along its shores. Earlier, warm south winds had brought gray overcast and scuds of low cloud, but by late afternoon the wind had died, leaving open stretches of mirror-smooth water. Only the trailing wakes of distant waterfowl marred the surface. Gentle wavelets licked the sandy shore.

Three bluebirds, startling bits of color, played about the stubby weed stalks at bankside, their blues and russets luminous against winter's somber browns. Two of them soon moved off but one remained, mounting the very top of a tall oak overlooking the water. As if moved by the tranquil mood and by the warmth of the spring evening, it began a subdued caroling. Softly, without opening its bill, it repeated the same three or four mellow notes, slurring upward or descending at the end of each phrase. The plaintive, tender quality of the bluebird's voice added somehow to the spirit of the day.

Suddenly the sky was filled with sound. A ragged *V* of migrating geese, honking bedlam, appeared over the trees to the south. As they approached

the expanse of West River, they fell into disarray. Some of them began a glide to the water; others tumbled awkwardly in an effort to drop quickly. But most of them broke ranks only momentarily, soon continuing on course to the northeast. Those that had hesitated and dropped toward the water recovered quickly and joined the others as they passed out of sight.

Following close behind the geese were about seventy-five swans, their wild whooping adding to the noise and confusion. They separated from the geese, changing direction slightly, but then moved off to the northeast as well, the clamor fading with them.

Minutes later, not a goose or swan was to be seen or heard. Their abrupt and noisy passage, in such contrast to the tranquil mood of the afternoon, seemed but an apparition, a fancy of the imagination.

Beverly Beach County Park

A passing front had brought showers through the night, but at dawn only a thin bank of cloud remained on the horizon. Above it swirled tatters of gray blue cirrus. With the sunrise, their undersides flushed a glowing pink.

Against the brightening sky, far out over the water, coursed scores of birds. Wheeling, circling, and crossing, there was no pattern to their movement. Gulls, they looked like, foraging or scavenging. But some among them were larger, with a peculiar, gliding flight pattern. Gannets! Birds of the open sea, the ocean. Here, halfway up the Chesapeake Bay!

They alternately flapped and soared on long, black-tipped wings, set far back on their bodies. The ample tail tapered, giving them a cross-shaped profile, pointed at all four extremities. With shallow wing beats, they stroked lightly, at times using only the tips of their wings. With an air and a grace quite distinctive, they circled and weaved, their gaze intent on the water below.

It was fish they were after. It was fish they had followed this far up the Bay. To catch them they plunged

powerfully into the water, sending up showers of white spray as they hit the surface. Upon spotting a fish, a gannet would angle its wings and fall at a downward slant, sometimes diving almost vertically. Using their wings and feet, they adjusted their position on the way down and struck the water with such force that they disappeared for seconds at a time.

Some of them moved closer to shore, many entering the narrower confines of West River. On those that were near enough, I could see the buffy head color and the large grayish blue bills. Except for the dark wing tips, their bodies were pure alabaster white.

Wintering in the southwestern Atlantic and nesting in the Canadian Maritimes, gannets would be migrating at this season. Their normal course would take them offshore along the coast; only stragglers would wander into sounds and estuaries. But these were not just a few stragglers. Hundreds of them had followed the spring run of anadromous fish (those that come to fresh water to spawn).

What was the attraction here, so far from their customary haunts? I asked a fisherman tending his nets just offshore what he was catching. "White perch and plenty of alewives!" It was probably the latter that the birds were after, since the alewives, like the gannets, had also come up from the ocean.

MARCH 21

Triton Beach

At 3:05 A.M. the tilt of the earth brought the sun in direct line with the equator, officially bringing spring to the Northern Hemisphere. Temperatures were mild, following a storm that moved in from the south with strong winds and heavy rain. White-caps rolled across the Bay and even in the smaller inlets and creeks. Extra-high tides washed over marshes and shorelines.

The warmth and moisture set the

stage for a strange and ancient drama, one that has played every spring since Paleozoic times, since before the age of the dinosaurs. Such conditions give the biological cues that initiate the courtship and mating of that mysterious and beautiful creature of darkness, the spotted salamander. The performance opens annually, often for just a one-night stand, on the first warm, rainy night of spring.

The theater this spring was a pocket-sized pond set in a second-growth woodland, just off a side road. Though wet enough to support a modest growth of cattails, it was dependent largely on rain water. It was to this temporary pool that the salamanders came to dance, to perform a timeless, primordial ritual. It is only on this mission, a few evenings a year, that they emerge from their underground lairs. They live beneath logs and in burrows during the rest of the year, rarely emerging except during these brief hours of mating and when they move over land toward breeding ponds. Even this short migration takes place under cover of darkness.

Act One had ended when I first came onto the scene. A shrill chorus of spring peepers had alerted me just past ten P.M. By then, salamanders had already made the trek from their winter quarters and were gathered at the pond. I saw the first one, poised at water's edge, in the shadowy beams of the flashlight—a dark-tinted, delicately marked lizardlike creature. Alert, with tiny legs extended, it stared back with large, protruding eyes set above a blunt, rounded snout. Handsomely marked with light yellow on grayish brown, it was close to nine inches long.

Within a few feet was another, partially submerged. Frightened by the light, it slithered away beneath the leaves and bottom debris. Others were visible every few feet, resting in the shallow margins. Most were tolerant and easily approachable.

Toward the center of the pool, at a depth of about a foot, a score of salamanders had converged in a writhing mass. The water rippled with their squirming undulations. Entwined, they caressed and nudged each other. Every minute or so, one would detach itself, wriggle to the surface and take a quick gulp of air, then drift back down. A group courtship, this seemed, with many males wooing one or two females.

Attached to leaves and twigs near all this activity were minute white capsules, knobbed at the tip. These I recognized as the spermatophores deposited by the males, on which rested the seminal fluid. The stimulated female squats on these structures, and with the lips of the cloaca, takes them in to fertilize her eggs. The

male's mission is to excite the female with his dancing, enticing her to approach and contact these spermatophores.

With all the commotion, it was difficult to see direct interaction between the sexes. Those standing on the water's edge, however, were obviously females. As soon as one moved into the water, it was approached by two or three males from the central melee. For a moment they floated motionless, facing her; then, twisting and rolling, the males spiraled and looped around her. Soon they all fell in with the whirling mass.

This primitive ballet was still in progress when I left, close to midnight. When I returned the next morning, not a salamander was to be seen. The white bases of the spermatophores littered the floor of the pool, but where were the salamanders? A mass of eggs the size of a tennis ball floated amid the vegetation, and another egg mass was attached to an underwater stem. But there was no trace of the salamanders. Had they left the pond and burrowed back into the earth, to remain for yet another year in the dampness, in the darkness in which they have thrived for 300 million years?

MARCH 22

Tuckahoe Creek

The March sun has been gradually warming the waters of the Chesapeake and the four hundred streams that feed its forty-eight tributaries. In a system so complex, with such varying degrees of depth and salinity, water temperatures range widely. The fresher, more shallow creeks warm first, weeks ahead of the saltier open Bay.

When these waters warm to about 45 degrees, the earliest fish begin their spawning runs. Yellow perch and shiners are the first to stir, moving upstream into shallower water. And there is no need for a thermometer to measure this threshold. When the time is right, the river banks will be crowded with fishermen.

Early this morning fishermen of all ages lined a bridge crossing the narrow upper reaches of this tributary of the Choptank. With water temperatures reaching close to 50 degrees, both yellow and white perch had begun their spawning runs. The yellow perch have been active here for the past ten days; white perch have just started to move in.

As one man lifted his rod with a yellow perch on the line, a gelatinous strand of eggs spilled along the shore. He mentioned that another perch he had caught earlier also dropped eggs. Nearby, bits of these jellylike ribbons, some several feet long, floated among downed branches.

The range of tints across the perch's body turned from bronze to olive green to washed-out gold. Vertical brownish bars were broken with random spotting, which showed hints of violet. The brillant lower fins, orange grading to vermillion, were set like gems in its pearly white belly. (Etymologists trace the word *perch* to the classical Greek *perkanos*, which means the dusky greenish yellow color of ripening figs or grapes.)

But the run of yellow perch was nearly over; now it was the time for white perch. The fishermen were catching them by the bucketful. Varying in size from six to ten inches, the largest white perch also dropped eggs as they were lifted from the water. Even the slight pressure of grasping the fish caused eggs to extrude from the genital aperture. The ripe eggs seemed to completely fill the body cavity, swelling the fish to plumpness.

Other creatures were also responding to the warming water. Down in the saltmarshes bordering the lower Bay, the first of the fiddler crabs had awakened. Dozens of them hastened over the clumps of exposed shore. They were mud fiddlers, the smallest of the three native species, with bright blue markings on their carapaces. Will they have to go back into hibernation? It won't stay this warm.

MARCH 26

West River to Cheston Creek, by canoe

Mild temperatures and an unusually high tide suggested a canoe trip, despite an overcast with rain imminent. Though it was midmorning, a mist still lay over the estuary; gentle swells felt their way across its surface.

Several thousand waterfowl had congregated, massed in the open Bay and sprinkled about the coves and inlets. Many were ruddy ducks, now sporting the bright russets of breeding plumage. Most floated aimlessly as they slept, heads tucked under their back feathers.

Much more active were the closely packed crowds of scaup, about one third of the entire flock. They took to the air in swift courtship pursuits, parties of them hurtling up and over the water in tight clusters, twisting and turning, zigging and zagging. Separate chases were continually beginning and ending. One exhausted hen hit the surface and dived underwater, her suitors immediately going down after her. Second laters she surfaced; her followers then bobbed up, widely scattered and looking for her. There was a mad scramble as they closed in. A skittering and splashing, and they were all airborne once more.

Nearer shore swam a dozen redbreasted mergansers. A lively party, all were preening, shaking their wings and scattering spray. Three were splendid drakes in full regalia with rakish double crests. One keeled over to preen its belly, flashing white and orange underparts and a bright carmine foot.

All at once hundreds of ruddies awoke, stirred, then began running over the water. Most of them resettled quickly, but within moments took off again. Their splashing and thrashing created a loud din, rising almost to a roar. More ducks took to the air, and those still on the water rapidly swam to one side or the other, opening a broad swathe through their midst.

It soon became apparent that something underwater was frightening the birds, approaching and chasing them from below. Whatever it was moved with exceptional speed, covering much territory rapidly and rousing ducks over wide stretches of water—but it never came to the surface.

An hour or so later, as I paddled back to the landing, a river otter swam directly toward me, passing fearlessly within a few feet. Abruptly it lunged to one side, snared a fish, then tossed it lightly to gain a better grip. Appearing then to notice me for the first time, it seemed more curious than afraid.

With a gruntlike snort, the otter rolled over and disappeared beneath the surf.

Minutes later, I heard the same sound from the shore. The otter was fearlessly watching me from a cavity that had eroded between overhanging roots. It dropped from view, then emerged from another hollow in the bank, took one more look at me, snorted again, and swam back into deep water.

Was it the otter that had raised such havoc among the waterfowl? The otter's diet, though primarily of fish, also includes amphibians, crustaceans, and birds. Perhaps all the earlier confusion had been but another example of its playful nature.

MARCH 27

Lyons Creek

The weeping willows, imported
from Eurasia, have responded to the
warming days earlier than have the
native willows. Weeks ago they turned
a rich amber, their great drooping
branches rising and falling like foun-
tains. Most of them prosper in the
gardens and yards where they were
planted; a few have escaped and taken
hold in wilder situations, where they
must face the ravages of wind and
tide.

It is the native black willow that
defines so much of the character of
the Chesapeake landscape. It scratches
out a shrubby living on sandy shores
and beachfronts, takes root in the
muck of tidal streams, and sprawls
over ditches that line the cornfields of
the Delmarva Peninsula. The largest
specimens flourish along sheltered
creeks and riverbanks, where they
have a slouching, scraggly picturesque-

ness. Its principal branches, gnarled
and knotty, often spring from the base
of the trunk at sharp angles. The most
brittle of trees, it is almost certain to
be maimed and scarred with jagged
stumps. Yet the crown is light and delicate.

Now, as the days lengthen, these
native willows are veiled with a gauze
of pale green. Their twigs glow a
bright mahogony, as if some incandes-
cent fluid coursed through them. It
is among the most vibrant of spring
colors. In a month or so, just as the
leaves reach maturity, the willows will
come to flower. The bright yellow,
pollen-bearing catkins will hang from
some trees, the seed-bearing catkins
from others. Both are formed of
closely packed individual flowers, protected by silvery scales.

In the female flower, these scales

develop into hairy fibers that help disperse the seeds in the wind and enable them to float on the water. In a few weeks, when the cottony seeds are shed, they will form a white scum in backwaters under branches or where the current is not too strong. They may even germinate while floating in this mass, tingeing the water's surface with green.

Another native willow lives along Chesapeake tributaries. Willows can be taxonomically complex, but I have identified it, judging from its wider leaves and the fluffy, cottony seeds, as the Carolina willow, though the Bay is not strictly within its natural range. Local manuals limit this tree to the upper Potomac valley; one describes it as common about the city of Washington. Perhaps the Carolina willow, like many other plants, has spread its range, following the course of the Potomac downstream.

This species was formerly known as Ward's willow, in commemoration of the early botanist Lester F. Ward, whose *Guide to the Flora of Washington, D.C., and Vicinity* was published in 1881. The plant was described from specimens he collected near Chain Bridge on the Potomac. Ward's guide did not include the maritime flora of the Chesapeake or that of the lower Potomac. He did, however, include records from Upper Marlboro on the Patuxent, which was reached, he wrote, "by a good road."

Sellman Creek

It was nearly dark when the trail led to the creek, where the light reflecting on the water, brighter even than the sky, seemed to prolong the dusk. In the chill, no birds called. Only the silken rustling of marsh grass marred the stillness.

A further stirring in the shadows! A dark, humped form moved back and forth. Up and down. Hardly ten yards distant, an otter was rubbing against the trunk of a downed tree. Strangely, it had not become aware of my presence. Its back arched against the tree, it wriggled vigorously, then fell to the ground, rolling over with the same scratching motion. Its actions, much like those of a domestic cat, seemed partly in play. Then, again in the manner of a cat, it lolled and stretched, extending its legs full-length.

Pausing to leave a scent, it disappeared beyond some intervening shrubbery. I heard a splash and the otter reappeared, swimming across an inlet. Near the far shore, it rolled and twisted in the water, emerging with what appeared to be a chunk of wood. Tossing this up in the air—again, like a playful kitten—it climbed onto a grassy tump then loped along the creek's edge, its humped back flowing sinuously.

A disturbance just offshore betrayed yet another otter, diving with vigor and abandon. Watching, I became aware that three otters were actively feeding together, emerging with fish then lunging back into the water with snakelike twists. Frequently they swam in the shallows, tails and backs exposed. More than once, one seemed to stand on its head, its thick tail sticking straight up out of the water. Twice, one rolled over on its back with a fish in its paws, to eat in sea-otter fashion. All were large, robust animals (though one was noticeably smaller), and all had wide grayish muzzles.

MARCH 30

Beverly Beach County Park

The ospreys had returned two weeks ago from their winter sojourn, probably somewhere in the Carribean. Three pairs now occupied the

beach front here, a stretch of several hundred yards. At times these big raptors can seem almost colonial, so tolerant are they of close neighbors.

Immediately upon arrival, they had set about the business of nesting. Two old nests were renovated: one on a telephone pole just up from the beach, and the other on an old duck blind a few yards offshore. And work had begun on a new nest atop a wind-damaged sweet gum tree, virtually overlooking the duck blind.

On two of the nests this morning females were sitting complacently. On the other, the offshore duck blind, stood three ospreys. A steady chatter flowed from this trio, with more than a hint of nervous irritation. Two were males, smaller and clear-breasted. This pair took flight at my approach, one of them gliding to a nearby piling. The other followed, piping in agitation, and hovered over his rival. The two then grappled, locking talons, their great wings flapping wildly as they fell into the water. They floated briefly, spread-eagled, then both flew off, rising from the water with no difficulty. The female remained on the nest during this fracas, murmuring excitedly, but quieted when her two suitors disappeared.

Ten minutes later, a lone male

mounted high into the clear blue sky, directly above the nest, screaming all the while. Several times he dropped fifteen or twenty feet, then rose again. Finally, he launched into one long, precipitous dive to the nest, where the female still waited. The two rested amicably, side by side. Had the matter been settled?

MARCH 31

Beverly Beach County Park

Apparently nothing had been resolved. The three ospreys were still hanging about the offshore nest, and, at times, all were on the nest together. There remained some tension, with brief flurries of petulant mewing, but not the aggressive hostility shown

yesterday. Again, one male rose very high and began the courtship display—a dipping, undulating flight punctuated with the high-pitched screaming. It held its position by fluttering merely the tips of its wings, while sounding its shrill cry. It held its body at an odd, perpendicular angle, its tail tilted toward the ground and spread wide. A half-eaten fish hung from the osprey's talons.

The female stood on the platform, continuing that anxious babble. The other male, out of sight, delivered a squealing whistle. Later the two males skirmished over a pond, maneuvering very long wings with remarkable dexterity.

APRIL 1

Flag Ponds County Park

A bright but saturated morning, a world washed clean after a heavy downpour during the night. A south wind, warm and smelling of rain and moistened earth, spiced the air with the fragrance of spring.

Wildflowers scented the woods along the Ridge Trail, overlooking the crowns of red maples in the swamp below. Bloodroot blossoms cascaded down a ravine, as thick and white as a snow drift. The flowers must have been brought to bloom by this morning's sun. The wind and rain last night would surely have torn off the delicate petals, since they fall at the slightest touch.

Atop the slope, the flowers of Dutchman's-breeches nodded among the feathery, sage green leaves. The petals formed a heart-shaped sack, which may or may not look like like the trousers worn by Dutchmen. But the name has a certain poetic flavor. Suppose they were called "Dutchman's pants"!

Trailing among the leaves were the pinkish veined petals of spring beauty, with narrow, grasslike leaves. Its mild aroma attracted an early bumblebee.

At midmorning, revived by the warmth, a large butterfly, dark with pale edges on its wings, floated erratically through the woods. A mourning cloak, it came to rest on the sunny side of a tree trunk where, in pausing, it was transformed. The dark color became a rich brown with maroon iridescence, and the pale edges turned into a delicate fringe of cream yellow bordered with spots of brilliant blue. When it raised its wings, bringing them together, the muted and striated pattern of the undersides matched the bark on which it rested.

The earliest of our butterflies to

appear, it had wintered in the adult stage, hibernating in a sheltered crevice or hollow tree. Most insects leave their spark of life in eggs that hatch the following spring; others overwinter as pupae in the safety of a cocoon or chrysalis. But this frail creature had endured the cold and ice of the past few months with no such protection.

Farther along the trail, bottom-land backwaters ran crimson with the fallen florets of the red maple. The starry bursts of stamens, their pollen spent, remained intact, forming a watery carpet. Carving dark trails through it were half a dozen wigeon, lovely in fresh plumage that combined subtle pinkish lavenders with irides-cent greens and accents of pure white and black. One drake splashed noisily as it bathed, vigorously rubbing its head against the back feathers, then running its bill through the pinkish lavender flanks. With the widgeon were other ducks: two pair of gadwall, the drakes with distinctively shaped heads, swam off to themselves. From any distance, they appeared a nonde-script gray, but their finely vermicu-lated plumage, so remarkably intricate, has a beauty appreciated only up close.

APRIL 2

Muddy Creek, by canoe

The water here is brackish, be-coming saltier near the mouth of the creek. Its headwaters remain quite fresh, despite the tides that sweep in from the Bay. The vegetation along its banks is an accurate gauge of salinity and now, in April, of the advancing season. Each plant in the marsh com-munity matures at a different rate.

The swirling tufts of salt marsh grass were today tinged at the base with the fresh green of spring. Groundsel bushes were leafing out, their buds a darker green, but the big cordgrass showed no sign as yet of the turning season, its six-foot stalks still pale and wintry sere.

Upstream, the mallow stems showed no sign of new life, but yel-low-green spears of young cattail were already a foot high. They stood in contrast to the dense stands of old growth, much of which still stood tall. But in places, last year's cattail stems had been severed cleanly, close to the water. Some had been cut at higher levels, and snippets of cattail floated, swirling in the current. In places, so much of the vegetation had been felled that wide swathes lay open through the marsh.

Ripples in the water betrayed the culprit. A swimming muskrat crossed, its mouth stuffed with fresh cattail leaves. Its eyes, twin black beads, showed just above the surface. Undulating behind was its tail, thin and rat-like, but flattened vertically. It paddled steadily downstream, then disappeared beyond a marshy island. There, in a more extensive clearing, were four muskrat houses—mounds of matted vegetation. Conical in shape, their construction was primarily of cattail shreds, with bits of smartweed and other flotsam filling the interstices. One lodge, only a few feet high, had its entire topside roofed with the tough, wiry stems of big cordgrass.

All the vegetation used for the lodges was brownish, old and deterio-rating; there was no sign of the fresh greens the animals were busily gathering. The recently cut stems may have been cached for later, or used to feed the young. There were indeed shredded remnants of green at the plunge holes used as doorways, a sign that the muskrats were feasting on the succulent young plant growth.

One large muskrat stood to its full height, grasping a cattail stalk with both feet. It gnawed through it in seconds and felled three more, then placed them together, roughly parallel. It grasped them as if to swim away, but found the load too cumbersome. This difficulty was apparently overcome by cutting the stems into sections, each about a foot long. Eventually it paddled off with all but one stalk and disappeared beneath the water.

Though the lodges were clustered

in a cleared portion of the marsh, I saw only two muskrats. Others may have been spending the daytime hours inside, resting or suckling young.

APRIL 3

Sheepshead Cove

Three full days of strong northwest winds had blown much water out of the Bay, leaving an exceptionally low tide. The creek, which flowed at less than half its normal width, was but a narrow rivulet trickling through soft ooze.

The mud was pitted with tracks, etched in sharp relief by the low angle of the late sun. I was able to identify the footprints of raccoons and otters, ducks and gulls. Tiny tracks belonged to a songbird, and larger ones with long toes were probably left by a rail. The otter tracks, almost circular and showing a bit of the webbing between the toes, were bunched and random, indicating a lot of activity in one place. Even imprints of the tail and belly showed. I could picture these playful creatures frolicking under last night's moon.

A boggy pasture that merged with the marsh brought to mind thoughts of snipe. Just the kind of habitat for them. Almost immediately one flushed in front of me, then dropped back in the grasses about twenty yards farther on. I carefully marked the spot and moved a bit closer, hoping to study it at close range, but grass and snipe had become as one. The chevroned ochres and tans of the bird became a part of the earth. The snipe had disappeared. Yet I knew there was still an eye glistening there somewhere, watching, waiting. Maybe I could catch the glint in that eye.

As I stood there in the bog, straining to find the snipe, I was gripped by the mood and spirit of the spring evening. A song sparrow tinkled, then gamboled off with a partner. A flicker offered a bit of its "wick-up" call (how this sound enlivens the deadness of winter!) and a cardinal whistled.

In the half-light of dusk, the dun colors of the marsh mingled in the eye, changing subtly with the very act of seeing. The gray brown of the groundsel bushes, the purplish brown of the marsh elders, and the yellow brown of the spartina were so close in value, the differences so subtle, that the optical mix resembled an impressionist painting. Open pools and sinuous runnels of water reflected these colors, with hints of blue from the sky above.

Where was that snipe? I took a few more steps, each one causing a sucking "swoosh" as I pulled a foot from the muck. Still, nothing stirred.

The bird must be just a few feet in front of me, I thought, unless it had sneaked away on foot. I felt that somewhere nearby, a dark eye was watching, a heart throbbing.

Closer.

Closer.

Another step, and up they jumped! Two snipe! A harsh call, like the snap of a camera's shutter, trailed after them. They crossed the pasture, circled back against the orange horizon, and disappeared.

APRIL 4

Otter Point Estuarine Park

It is not green, but yellow, that brightens the bottom lands these early days of spring. The golden flowers of the spicebush emerge before the unfolding of leaves or buds, before even the early wildflowers. Willows and alders have developed catkins, but they are not yet really in bloom.

So, for a few fleeting days, the spicebush has its time in the sun. The starry clusters of blooms arranged along the stem create a light of their own, all the more startling for the stark bareness around them. Within a week they will be lost amid the bursting new foliage.

The downy flowers resolve through the hand lens into shiny, greenish sepals. There are no petals. It is the large, yellow anthers, hanging on long, drooping stamens that impart the golden glow. Nodding on these filaments, the twin anthers look like the eyes of space creatures in a Hollywood production. Growing on separate trees, the female (pistillate) flowers are not as showy. All parts of the shrub have a lemony fragrance.

APRIL 5

Thomas Point

The early sun swam in an amorphous sea of cloud, fog, and water. Then, with the clearing of the atmosphere, the Bay lay calm to the horizon, reflecting a rose gray sky. Scanning with the scope, I could make out waterfowl scattered over the entire field of view. Many were apparently feeding on the bottom, diving vigorously. Others took brief, skittering flights, then ploughed back into the water. Some appeared to be resting or sleeping.

Bunched companies of buffleheads, flickering black and white, dipped and swerved over the water. In some form of nuptial pursuit, they splashed down briefly, then reappeared and were off again. Rafts of scaup, their numbers augmented by newly arrived migrants from farther south, rocked in the light chop of the waves. A few canvasbacks, with lighter backs and rusty heads, floated among the scaup. Of the thousands that had wintered here, most had already left for the northwestern prairies.

The trim little buffleheads were charged with energy. A verve and vigor characterized their every action. One could recognize them merely by the splashing and commotion that preceded and ended their aerial chases. These encounters seemed sexually motivated, with several males after a lone female. Larger groups, of six to eight birds, included several females and their chases may have been more in the spirit of play. After

fifty or a hundred yards, twisting and turning in midair, they skidded into the water, pink feet splayed like water skis. In most instances, they dived immediately. But at times the drakes remained on the surface, bobbing their heads, raising their crest feathers, and swimming toward a hen.

Goldeneyes—heavier, stockier ducks—remained on the water but assumed odd mating postures, heads pumping or thrown back over rumps. Low, rasping sounds from off the water seemed to come from these displaying ducks.

By midmorning the overcast had burned off. Just offshore, resplendent in the sun, swam a horned grebe, now in full breeding plumage after having spent a winter in somber gray. The rusty hues of its neck and sides, glistening with droplets of moisture, were strikingly complemented by black cheeks and crown, and by a creamy patch behind the eye. Projecting from each side of the head were tufts of gold, the so-called horns. The dark cheeks were puffed, giving the head an oversized, distinctive shape. Its fiery red eyes burned with jewel-like intensity. Not far off, another horned grebe, diving briskly, was still in winter dress. Not one bright feather. But it had those same incredible eyes.

While I was watching these two, yet another grebe appeared, this one in flight. Struggling to keep aloft, it soon dropped weakly into the water. In the air it had held its neck awkwardly low, and this posture, combined with the short wings and trailing legs, had presented a form almost grotesque. So inept do they look while flying, one wonders at the distances they travel. They, too, breed primarily in the prairie provinces.

APRIL 6

Mayo Beach

A sullen, chilly day, with no sun at all, did not dampen the spirits of a brown thrasher, just returned from a winter in the South. It mounted the very top of a pondside sweet gum, a touch of russet against the leaden sky, and for half an hour it sang in subdued, almost whispered cadence.

In carefully measured phrases, the notes fell as if the singer were composing as it sang. Slurred trills and whistles, each given twice, were accented with a variety of clucks and whistling sounds. The leisurely, unhurried delivery enhanced the impression that the performance was more than instinctive, that some creative force was at work. Would such a close relative of the mockingbird have the skill (and the tendency) to improvise, to make choices?

Pausing in its migration, the bird was not singing to attract a mate. Nor was it advertising or protecting territorial rights. There seemed no further incentive than to please itself, to express pure joy on an April morning. And there seemed to be an element of freedom, of choice in its song. (Such conjecture would be anathema to the behaviorists, who deny that birds have any aesthetic sense at all, that their songs have a purely biological function.)

The singing of the thrasher this morning brought to mind another bird song. It recalled a nightingale, heard long ago near the medieval German town of Heidelberg. I remember that, at the time, the nightingale reminded me of the brown thrasher back home. When I heard the careful phrasing, the sweetness of tone, and the impassioned delivery of the European bird, I was transported for an instant across the sea, to springtime on the Chesapeake, to the land of the brown thrasher.

APRIL 7

Sellman Creek

Fluttering weakly, its legs hanging limp, a woodcock flushed from the trail along the creek. It flew with its body at an odd, unnatural angle, the tail depressed awkwardly, so that the bird seemed sick or injured. It settled a dozen yards away and began thrashing about nervously among the leaves. The tail was fanned and elevated, displaying the contrast of black and white tips and the rusty undercoverts.

Falling for the ruse, I followed

after the "injured" bird. As it continued flopping about, wings aquiver, I realized I had been fooled: the old broken-wing trick. She was leading me away from her nest.

So I retreated to where I had first disturbed her, hoping to find either chicks or eggs. No luck. Too carefully hidden and too well camouflaged. During my search, I could hear the distressed parent nearby, uttering a low, bleating note. She continued to feign injury, feebly flapping one wing.

I resumed my way along the trail, but had not gone more than a hundred yards when another woodcock broke cover. During the short flight, its body and tail were again held in that strange tilted position. And again she hobbled about on the ground with half-extended wings.

Not deceived this time, I stopped in my tracks. Looking down at my feet, I saw that I had nearly stepped on the chicks: four of them, still in fluffy down. Distinctly marked with dark brown on a buffy ochre ground, they blended magically with the surrounding leaf litter. Had they kept still and quiet, they would have been nearly invisible. But they were peeping in high, shrill tones and actively moving their heads and surprisingly stubby bills. When my eyes strayed briefly, it

took a few moments to relocate them—even though they were within a few feet and I knew precisely where they were. Not wishing to disturb them further, I moved away, taking care where I stepped.

Later, almost in darkness, the susurrant murmur of woodcock wings fell from the sky: the sound of a woodcock in courtship flight. When this soft fluttering ceased, there followed almost immediately a twittering of liquid chirps and warbles as the bird descended. A spectral, mothlike shape dropped beyond the trees, falling from sight.

Then a strange, buzzing "beep" emanated from the shadows. This calling continued for several minutes at regular intervals until the woodcock took to the air, rising in a gradual plane against the twilight. At two hundred feet, the whispering of wings began once more, continuing as the batlike form hovered and circled. And again came the enchanting climax: that singing, musical descent.

I managed to follow the ghostly shape to earth and, through binoculars, watched as he repeated the buzzing call, given each time with a convulsive, shaking effort. Within hearing distance, yet another woodcock was sky dancing.

This turn of affairs set me to wondering. Since the females here had already produced broods, were there others in the area that had not yet mated? It is known that this species has but one brood a year, though renesting will occur if the first attempt meets with failure. Was there a population of drifting, opportunistic males still looking for mates? Biologists believe the woodcock to be polygamous.

Or perhaps (and this seemed more likely) the evening flight may not in all instances be related to courtship and mating.

APRIL 10

Beverly Beach County Park

A visit here late in the day confirmed the strange polyandrous relationship among the ospreys first observed on March 30. All three birds, two of them males, stood placidly on the nest platform, their white breasts reddened by the setting sun. Major differences seemed to have been reconciled.

They did not, however, stay to roost together on the nest. As the dusk deepened, both males flew off, finding perches high in nearby trees.

One was dramatically silhouetted against the light at the horizon.

Rare instances of polygynous ospreys—one male breeding with two females—are on record. In one study involving 190 nests, there were three such trios. In each case two separate nests were involved, close enough for the male to defend both. So, on occasion, two females will occupy one nest with a single male. But there seems to be no record of a relationship like this one: two males sharing one nest with one female.

This can possibly be attributed to the large local population of ospreys. (A study estimated 3,700 pairs nest by Chesapeake waters.) With so many ospreys there may simply be a shortage of suitable nesting sites.

APRIL 11

Jug Bay Wetlands Center

Unlike the names given to birds, those of butterflies are often as lovely as the creatures themselves. As opposed to birds named "sharp-shinned hawk," "old squaw," or "yellow-bellied sapsucker," we have the "dreamy dusky-wing," the "pearl crescent," and the "tawny emperor." Another happy and appropriate name has been given one of our earliest butterflies, the spring azure.

A bit of color in a world still winter-drab, the tiny azure seems a creature from another world. With wings of purest blue, it emerges into a landscape of withered brown and muted gray. Early this afternoon, four of these elfin gems hovered about a woodland puddle. Like violets taken to wing, they fluttered restlessly, settling in pairs, then spiraling upward together. Separating, they fell back to earth, alighting by the moisture. When one moved close to another, they were off again.

Coming to rest with wings closed, showing only the undersides, the azures became less conspicuous. The pale underwings, ashen gray with finely sprinkled dark spots, effectively camouflaged them. Their black eyes, disproportionately large and rimmed with yellow, glistened with a light that would burn but a few days. For spring azures are short-lived; the females emerge and mate on their first day, lay eggs on the second, and rarely survive a third or fourth.

Merkle Wildlife Management Area

Johnny-jump-up is a popular name given the little violets now springing up in pastures and open woodlands here. Also known as field pansies, they are of uncertain ancestry and questionable lineage. At least two species are certainly of European origin, and some taxonomists, citing common characteristics, believe that none is native to this land.

But I like to think that at least one of the group is a true American. Its scientific name, *Viola rafinesquii*, commemorates an early naturalist who visited the Chesapeake. Born in Turkey, Constantine Rafinesque came to this country in 1802, and in 1804 his botanical travels brought him to Chestertown and Easton on Maryland's Eastern Shore. During the same year, he studied the plants along the Susquehanna near Havre De Grace.

A wild eccentric, Rafinesque discovered and described so many new species that he lost credibility with most of the scientists of his time. However, many of his finds that were at first rejected were verified decades or even a century later.

Viola rafinesquii, one of the few

annuals among the violets, shows up regularly but unpredictably in the sandy open areas around the Bay. Its flowers vary from cream to blue violet and are usually tinged with yellow. Most distinctive are the leaves, which taper into the stalk, at which juncture grow the lobed stipules, cleft like a cock's comb.

APRIL 13

Deep Creek

A north wind had lowered temperatures into the thirties, but the morning was cloudless, the atmosphere startling in its clarity. The far shore of the Bay, often hidden in haze, lay crisp and clear on the horizon.

A whirling mass of white across the pond resolved through the binoculars into a tumult of feeding gulls and terns. Schooling fish, trapped in the shallows by the ebbing tide, provided easy pickings. Bits of silver flashed amid the splash and spray as the feeding birds hovered and plunged.

Immaculate in fresh plumage, these Forster's terns were likely pausing on migration, en route to the Prairie Provinces. Hanging in the wind, bills directed downward, they hurtled headlong into the water, usu-ally to emerge with fish wriggling in their orange red beaks.

The Bonaparte's gulls among them were likewise in midjourney. (This week marked the main thrust of their migration). Unlike the terns, they are not anatomically designed to catch fish. But they were drawn to the bounty and scrambled after the fish, some of which were flopping about in the ebbing shallows. Dozens of these trim, delicate gulls hovered just above the water, trailing coral red feet. A herring gull nearby seemed, in comparison, bulky and clumsy.

The tide continued to fall, driven by the northwest wind, and soon half of the pond was glistening, oozy mud. Taking advantage of this new shoreline, many of the gulls and a few terns took a break from fishing, settled on the flats, and immediately began to preen and bathe. Sheltered from the wind here, about three hundred birds had soon congregated, with much lively flutter and spray. A pearly gathering against tawny brown.

Within minutes, they all rose at once, a feathered snowstorm, collectively emitting a low, cackling gabble. They used the force of the wind, letting it take them over the marsh in a wide circle. Breasting the breeze, they immediately fell back to the same resting spot. Across the salt meadow between the pond and the Bay, a harrier veered just over the tallest grasses.

Pennington Pond

When first heard amid the dawn chorus, I thought the plaintive notes were a fragment of the white-throated sparrow's spring song. Yet they breathed the clarity, the timbre of thrush music. Much subdued, the effect was entrancingly ventriloquistic. Was it issuing from the depths of a nearby holly? Or did it come from the woods across the marsh? Or were there two birds?

Eventually I located the singer, surprisingly close, hidden in a tangle of honeysuckle. Tawny, autumn-colored leaves persisting on the vine partially obscured it. For ten minutes the bird lingered, all the while offering these dulcet whisperings. Its spotted breast was facing me, and its wings were lowered to its flanks, so I could see the throat vibrate with the sound: sustained single notes, interspersed with half-warbles spiraling up the scale.

Was it this warm, sun-filled morning, rich with the promise of spring, that inspired this transient hermit thrush to song? Far from its summer home in the North, it did not give the full-throated outpouring heard there, but rather a soft, suppressed version. The pitch seemed lower than the normal range for this thrush, the length of the figures longer. But the overall pattern was typical: one introductory note followed by shorter phrasings, each a bit higher than the last. And there was that distinctive flutelike quaver or tremolo.

The thrush turned about, raising, then lowering, its fox red tail. The rusty feathers of the lower back and rump fell in soft, bunched masses. Once more it sang, but only briefly, then dropped to the ground, where it poked about among the leaves. Soon it was back to a holly tree, near the place I had first found it. And did I hear once more its faint fluting?

49

Hill's Bridge

Dark clouds tumbled low across the morning sky, following a windy front that had brought rain most of the night. Wraiths of driven mist veiled the river shore, blending the yellowish haze of willow with the

tawny red of maple. Other bankside vegetation merged in a formless mass of pastel green.

Even brighter green were the patches of sweet flag, or calamus, emerging from the tidal flats and the adjacent lowlands. The only green showing in the winter-browned marsh, it was already six to ten inches high; by midsummer, it will have disappeared in a fecund wetland jungle.

Its swordlike leaves grew in bunches joined at the base, where they attached to the underground rhizome. At this juncture, the green turned into a rich, purplish red. A young couple on the bank, fishing for white perch, collected a basket of these leaves. "To use in salad," they explained, and showed me the tender young leaves unfolding in the center of the stalk.

The whole plant has a spicy, aromatic flavor and smell. The roots were used by Native Americans as both a seasoning and a main dish, and candied calamus was a favorite confection among the early settlers. The flower, which will not appear until midsummer, is a thumblike spathe, projecting sideways from a leaf. Few of these flowers develop, possibly because the plant spreads so readily from the rhizome.

By midmorning, swatches of blue showed through the clouds, the sunlight bringing to life bands of swallows that swooped over the river, lifting into the wind, dancing and pirouetting in midair. Three kinds rushed past: barn swallows, tree swallows, and rough-winged swallows, the last being larger and paler than the others. All passed in a northward orientation, so most of them were likely on migration.

But many of the barn swallows were already at home. With much flutter and chatter, they came to rest on the supports under a highway bridge. One pair reclaimed a nest built last year, still intact, sheltered beneath a beam.

A couple of tree swallows, glistening with iridescent blue greens, paused briefly atop the bare stems of a mallow. Barn swallows rested, too, on these same mallow stems, alighting with a dainty butterfly gesture, arching slender, tapering wings above their backs. Lingering to preen, they struck balletic poses to reach the rump feathers.

The ebbing tide left wide flats exposed along the river shores and its marshy tributaries. Dabbling in this almost liquid mud was a party of ducks, nearly two dozen of them. Half

were green-winged teal, with chocolate heads and subtly spotted orange chests. Though still far from their nesting grounds, they were already paired off. The drakes closely attended the hens, leaping to the air in short flights to keep near them.

The others were wood ducks, also in a courting mood and already nesting. One drake stood on the roof of a nesting box, peering into the entrance hole where his mate had disappeared. Later, he flew to join her when she dropped to the water. Other woodies, obviously paired, dabbled in the watery mud.

On higher land, overlooking the river, mud turtles were crawling along the sandy roads searching for nesting sites. Two had finished laying, their carapaces still covered with soil. Another was in the early stages of burrowing. Predators had already found and destroyed several clutches, leaving the white shells broken and strewn about.

Stirred by the afternoon warmth, a tiny ruby-crowned kinglet broke into subdued bits of song. Barely audible at first, this virtuoso performance increased in volume and tempo, then trailed off at the end, the notes cascading over each other. Then, just as the measure seemed to be ending, more music bubbled forth, as if the finale had been momentarily forgotten. Was he lonely? Was he dreaming of his home in the Canadian spruces? Or was he merely singing to himself—a song of spring?

Toward dusk, as the sun set beyond the marshes, a great blue heron labored slowly downstream. Quite innocently, it blundered too close to an osprey nest set on a platform over the water. For this indiscretion, it was set upon by the ospreys, which twice drove the heron into the water, where it thrashed about awkwardly before managing to retreat.

APRIL 16

Shoreham Beach

The mass movements of migrating birds normally pass unnoticed. They either fly by night or at heights that render them nearly invisible. Mysteriously, the woods and waters are alive with birds that were not there the day before. But at times we can watch the passage of the day-flying species— seabirds, waterfowl, and raptors—and become aware of the scale, the spectacle of this seasonal ebb and flow across the face of the earth.

Times like this morning. At sun-rise, horizontal layers of cloud, lit from below, glowed a purple crimson. Against this light, flocks of flying birds were silhouetted, moving to the north.

Very high in the sky, almost at the limit of sight, cruised a compact flight of ducks. At that height and distance, they were but a pulsating mass that extended like an amoeba, first in front, then at the rear. At a lower level wavered a thin line, a threadlike wisp of waterfowl, barely visible. Closer were flocks of twenty-five to fifty birds, an endless stream of them. These were diving ducks, most likely scaup. I guessed that five thousand had passed by within half an hour.

Just offshore, clusters of Bonaparte's gulls coursed by in light, buoyant flight, just above the waves. Smartly clad in crisp dark hoods, their wings semaphored black and white. On they came. For more than an hour they passed, a ribbon unraveling against the morning sky. Taking a course to the northwest, they turned and moved up the South River. The instinct that was driving them would eventually take them to their nesting grounds in northwestern Canada and Alaska. Stragglers continued to pass by until midmorning.

The sky palpitated with birds.

Here, small winged triangles crossed against the light; there, pairs and singles careened over the water. A loon appeared above the gulls, its legs trailing behind, its neck extended and lowered. It looked strangely cross-shaped, the body as long as the wingspread. Two more loons followed, then a closely massed bevy of red-breasted mergansers, the drakes flickering black, white, and orange.

More loons, in twos and threes, loomed over the water; then came a squadron of ten. From 8:45 until 9:30 at least one hundred loons migrated past, some quite high and overland to the west. A contingent of horned grebes showed up, beating weakly just over the surf. Legs trailing, necks hanging clumsily, they looked exhausted and soon splashed down. Joining the procession were three Caspian terns—large, rangy birds with thin, tapering wings—and troupes of cormorants, dark and gooselike.

Landbirds, too, were using the Bay as a navigational landmark. A sharp-shinned hawk came to rest briefly on a cedar, then continued up the Bay. Four flickers flushed reluctantly from a grassy beach, not normal wood-pecker habitat; they were tired nearly to exhaustion. At least three Savannah sparrows, night migrants, crept through the same grasses. A single snowy egret leisurely flapped by, along with the season's first green-backed heron.

Both continued along the shore to the north.

The smooth surface of the Bay was marred by dark, undulating streaks: rafts of waterfowl. Most of them were scaup, squat diving ducks that use this part of the Chesapeake as a preparatory gathering place before resuming their northward journey.

I revisited the scene in the afternoon. It seemed another world. In the full light of midday, all migratory movement had ceased; the stage was empty, lifeless after that intense drama against the sunrise.

APRIL 17

Glebe Creek

The first botanist to probe the shores of the Chesapeake was John Clayton, a colonist born in England. Indeed, he was among the pioneers in the study of North American plants. As Clerk of the Court of Gloucester County, Virginia, he lived most of his life in Bay country. He added to his duties as clerk those of plant collector and explorer. Clayton corresponded with and sent plants to the great Carolus Linnaeus and was the author of *Flora Virginicus*, published in 1736. Among the plants he sent to

Linnaeus was the shrub we know today as the shadbush. So the first specimen known to science may well have come from the shores of the Chesapeake.

Linnaeus recognized only one kind of shadbush. Since his time, botanists have been busy splitting the genus. A recent treatise on Maryland trees, for instance, lists eight varieties, most of them quite difficult for the average person to classify.

Growing together today at the edge of a cattail marsh were two kinds of shadbushes. One plant had finished blooming, was nearly in full leaf, and had well-developed fruit. The other was in full bloom with its leaves still unfurled.

The petals of its flowers were about three-quarters of an inch long. Thin and spidery, they were a bit longer than those of the earlier flowers. The leaves, still folded, were light and furry, like little mouse ears. On the upper surfaces were tinges of wine red. Two pairs of long, antennalike stipules joined at the base of the leaves, which were finely toothed. Dark brown blotches marked their reddish stems.

The adjacent shadbush, with its leaves fully opened, had already set fruit. The pomes hung on drooping stems, looking much like rose hips (to which they are related). Reddish now, they will turn blackish purple when ripe. A calyx of five reflexed sepals persisted, adding a delicate and decorative touch.

APRIL 18

Marumsco Creek, by canoe

This was loblolly pine country. Groves of lofty, mature specimens, eighty to a hundred feet tall, lifted pagodalike crowns above a flat, open marshscape. Loblollies alone broke the monotony of the horizon. Pure stands of them covered abandoned fields and crowded alongside tidal guts. Offshore winds sighed through their thickly bunched foliage, giving life and movement to a landscape some might call lonely, even desolate.

On the upper reaches of this stream, pines marched right down to the waters edge—or until they got their feet wet in the fringe of shrubby swampland. Twisted branches hung over the water. Brushing by them in the canoe released a fragrant incense. At this season, the loblollies seemed to glow with an inner light. Adorning the tips of branches, lifted like candlabras, were clusters of staminate flow-

ers bright with pollen. Where the pollen sacs had split, the golden powder covered the terminal twigs. At the slightest touch, smoky puffs of yellow drifted off with the wind.

The wet thickets beneath the loblollies were still a tawny ochre, but they too were awakening to spring. The white blossoms of the chokeberry were just coming to flower. On only a few plants had the five delicately fringed petals opened, but others were in delicate green bud, ready to burst. Red fruits from last year had persisted through the winter. Across distant fields, a pale film of green misted a hardwood forest, with hints of red where the maples were in flower. The emerald green of sprouting wheat cloaked the cultivated land between.

A carpet of rose pink covered the approach to a bridge. Prospering a long way from their native Europe were the flowers of stork's-bill, a tiny wild geranium. Each flower was small, even insignificant, but in profusion they blanketed the roadside. Through the hand lens, the five carmine petals dangled over five burnt orange anthers in perfect symmetry. The long yellow sepals, striped with dark green, were covered with fine white hairs, as were the finely cut leaves. Some dis-

played, along with their flowers, the fruits that give the plant its name, shaped much like the bill and head of a stork.

I nearly missed seeing the muskrat. Partially hidden under the bridge, it grasped a willow branch and was gnawing the greening twigs extending from it. Its dried fur shone a rich, lustrous brown. With quick, skillful gestures, the willow was shuffled between its jaws and whiskered face. It paid me no attention at first, but then, uneasy at being watched, it nosed into the stream and swam off to a grassy tussock, dragging the branch along with it.

Unafraid there, it continued to gnaw the willow. The dark eyes showed none of the restless tension, the nervous mistrust so common to wild things. Here was a creature at home, adapted to its surroundings, attuned to the recurring ritual embracing the world around it.

APRIL 19

Nanticoke River

Life beneath the waters of the Chesapeake is charged with the same migratory urges as is that above the surface. Indeed, the seasonal travels of fish seem driven by instincts even stronger than those of the birds in the sky. In spring, the rivers and streams of the Bay pulsate with fish moving upstream from saltwater to spawn, many of them coming from the ocean. Others travel shorter distances, merely moving upstream from deep water winter quarters.

Before dams were erected blocking their way, herring made the trek from the sea, up the Bay, and then far inland. Some managed to make it up the Susquehanna into New York State; others followed the James and the Potomac to the foothills of the Blue Ridge. Yet others were content to spawn as soon as they reached fresh water.

and blueback herring, collectively known as "river herring." To the unpracticed eye, the two species are quite similar. Silvery gray with iridescent glints of yellow-green and pink, the two share a dark shoulder spot.

Scientists monitor these underwater movements by sampling the catches of commercial fishermen. Microscopic examination of scales can determine the age of a fish and the number of times it has spawned. Early today, I joined two biologists from the Department of Natural Resources in their investigations of pound nets on the Nanticoke, one of the most productive rivers in the Chesapeake system and still relatively free from industrial and agricultural pollution.

Each haul of the net, which took three men to draw and lift, brought in several dozen to a hundred fish. The bulk of the catch consisted of alewives

The bluish back of the one distinguishes it, as does the slightly larger eye of the alewife. There are other, internal differences.

Both species reach maturity at sea and return to their natal waters to spawn in the upper Bay and its major tributaries. Alewives prefer calmer, slower moving streams, but both species will follow the smallest of streams to their very source, even to places where the flow is but a few feet wide.

All those caught today were close to the same size, about a foot long, and three to four years old. Most of the alewives were "spent," having arrived several weeks ago, spawned, and already embarked on their way back to deeper water. The bluebacks were still "ripe" and their sex could be determined as they released either pinkish eggs or whitish milt.

Each haul of the net included a few large striped bass, better known in Bay country as rockfish. In one catch, half a dozen thrashed about. Measuring close to thirty inches or more, some were still gravid but most had already spawned.

We found striped bass eggs later, farther up the river in fresher water near Broad Creek. The eggs were suspended in smooth, oily slicks, which drifted on the surface. Semibouyant, they were kept afloat by tides and currents. Noisy splashings in the shallows nearby, with the occasional flash of a silver fin, were called "fights" by the fishermen. In these encounters—actually courting maneuvers between several males and a female—the eggs were fertilized.

Only a few American shad showed up in the nets. Once the most commercially valuable fish on the Bay, their present numbers are but a meager remnant of their former abundance. In Maryland, a protective moratorium was placed on catching them in 1980; Virginia did not give them legal protection until 1993. These efforts, along with restocking and the removal of barriers, have offered promising results.

Small numbers of catfish, both channel and white, were netted. They will not spawn until the summer months, when the water temperatures reach 70 degrees. They form a significant portion of the nonmigratory fish population. Three channel cats formed the entire catch of an angler I talked to later.

A few longnose gar were included in each draw of the net. Because they damage the nets and supposedly prey on young game fish, they are considered nuisances. But gar are worthy of interest. Living fossils, they have somehow survived since Eocene times, fifty million years ago, and have changed little since: a slender, toothed beak tapers into a long, cylindrical body covered with small diamond-shaped plates, "ganoid" scales, quite unlike those of other fish.

One haul of the net exposed two squirming, mucous-covered eels, creatures whose mysterious wanderings have puzzled and fascinated humans since the days of Aristotle. Migrating from fresh to salt water to breed, the adult females find their way to the sea, where they are joined by the males. Together, they make their way to the Sargasso Sea, in the South Atlantic, where they spawn. Newly hatched eels drift north with the gulf stream, then metamorphose into three- or four-inch elvers and begin long, arduous treks to fresh water. They are known to wriggle over dams and

through moist grass to bypass barriers. Whatever the force or reason that drives them inland, the females remain in fresh water until they reach adulthood, in four to eight years.

A side jaunt up Barren Creek brought us to a mudflat where the lowering tide revealed a series of funnel-shaped fyke nets, set primarily for black crappie. The nets held half a dozen ten-inch fish, congregating here to scrape nests in the muddy bottom. The male will guard the nest and the fry.

APRIL 20

Wakefield, Virginia

Our first president was born not far from the confluence of the Potomac River with the Chesapeake Bay, at Pope's Creek. Atop a bluff overlooking a wide reach of water, the estate commands a view across island-studded marshes to the river beyond. It is a prospect considerably more imposing than that from Mount Vernon, or from Ferry Farm, another Washington home on the nearby Rappahannock.

On this balmy spring day, 264 years later, the vista had probably not changed significantly. Ponderous oaks still lined the shoreline, their massive trunks and limbs not yet hidden by foliage. The marshes, still a wintry gray brown, swept away toward a lonely stretch of sandy beach. Massive red cedars covered one promontory and lifted dark spires from high places in the marsh. Along wooded shorelines, the deep magenta of redbud mingled with the white of black haw bloom.

But no longer were there the swarms of wildfowl that the youthful George Washington would have known. Three lone mergansers fished offshore and a family group of black ducks swam in the shadows of a distant backwater. On a sandy shoal, a single yellowlegs tiptoed among half a dozen dozing gulls. Otherwise, the broad stretches of water basked empty, lifeless in the warming sun. Washington had written of the swarms of ducks and geese that "clouded the skies" at Pope's Creek.

Closer, just across a cove from the Washington home, an eagle struggling with a large fish settled awkwardly in the topmost branches of a pine. His mate screamed a greeting from atop a bulky mass of sticks, her beak pointed skyward. Later, another eagle, a dark immature, coursed over a fallow field a few miles to the north. Its shadow passed near three fox cubs playing at the mouth of their den. At the first whiff of my approach, they disappeared.

Butterflies, newly emerged, fluttered restlessly through the budding woodlands adjacent to the homestead. A hatch of falcate orangetips danced restlessly over the forest floor. The males, white with corners of bright orange on their forewings, patrolled a narrow territory. One of them paused at a chickweed flower, moved hastily to a tuft of violets, then lingered about a cultivated viburnum. It repeated the same circuit, revealing the delicate marbling on the underwing when it touched down. The slightly larger females lacked the orange, but showed the same protective coloration under the wing.

Watching these fragile creatures in the spring sunshine, I wondered how their species had survived. Their wings seem mere bits of gauze, barely attached to slender and delicate bodies. And so ephemeral! The females will live four days at the most, the males a bit longer. Yet they have produced countless generations, through unnumbered centuries, enduring harsh winters, predation, parasites, and disease. Young George Washington surely watched the ancestors of the orangetips present today.

APRIL 21

Patuxent River County Park

A wood duck hen, disdaining several nest boxes erected nearby, chose instead to nest in a natural cavity. She hid her eggs in a hollow formed where a sycamore branch had broken off. The site was alongside a swampy backwater pond several miles from the main course of the river.

Greg Kearns, the naturalist at Patuxent River Park, discovered her secret. He had been carefully monitoring the nest boxes and had spent hours watching the birds from a blind. He first saw her fly up and cling to the edge of the nest hole, her tail propped against the trunk like a woodpecker's. In the days that followed, he watched her enter the cavity each morning, usually leaving within an hour. She was apparently laying an egg each day.

During these rest breaks, she consorted with other wood ducks that frequented the pond, preening, loafing, and feeding. No drakes ever entered the cavity, though one often perched in the lower branches of the nest tree.

When she began incubating after the clutch was complete, there was a marked change in her behavior. She would leave twice a day and fly off into the woods, disappearing for about an hour. Always she returned warily and with great caution.

Late on the 28th, the twenty-sixth day of incubation, the ducklings began to pip their eggs, accompanied by the low murmuring of their mother.

For the first time since incubation had begun, she broke her silence.

Once the pipping begins, it normally takes twenty-four to thirty hours for the young to work their way out. So Greg had watched for the hatching, knowing that the ducklings would leave the nest the day after. He wanted to record on film the dramatic moment when they jumped from the nest to the water below. He invited me to join him in the blind.

We were there before dawn, which became only a brightening grayness in an overcast. But the hen had already left the nest. As the light improved we found her back among the tangle of branches overhanging the shoreline. After preening quietly for half an hour, she swam toward the nest tree, cautious and alert. Something did not suit her, and she moved back among the underbrush. At the nest, there was nothing stirring, not a peep.

Another period of quiet—nearly an hour. Once more she approached the nest, clambering over some downed logs, then paused to rest, her belly pressed close to her perch. She tilted her head to watch a crow pass overhead. Again, an interval of repose. She seemed relaxed and tranquil, with no sign of the concern, of the anxiety that must have been simmering within her.

The climax was approaching, the moment for which the order of her life had been designed. All of her instincts—mating, egg-laying, the long days of incubation—were directed towards this one end: the procreation of her kind.

Finally, she fluttered to the water below the nest tree and, looking up, called to the young—the same soft murmur she used while brooding them. The response was immediate: a steady, almost frenetic peeping issued from the nesting cavity. A downy yellow head appeared at the entrance, and, with no hesitation, the duckling launched into space. With a flapping motion of its stubby wings, it splashed into the water, light as a powder puff.

Two more heads appeared at the

opening, then both plunged together, propelling themselves outward with a hopping motion. It obviously took considerable effort for them to gain the rim of the opening, as we could see them scrambling for a toehold and at times falling back in.

The three ducklings joined their mother, and were soon met by a fourth. Number five hesitated, taking its first look at the outside world, but then bravely leapt, pushing off with its webbed feet. The hen led this first contingent back into the marshy vegetation at the shoreline.

The next three that splashed down swam toward one another until they heard the peeping of the others and followed after them. Three more left the nest, one falling awkwardly onto the muddy bank. Two more jumped together, their feet waving frantically as they fell. Within five minutes, fifteen little wood ducks had made it safely to the water and were struggling to keep up with their mother.

APRIL 22

Wye Island

Most of the fungi, especially the mushrooms, appear with the first warm rains of autumn. Then, suddenly, where there was none the day before, rises the familiar stalk and gilled cup of the agarics. Puffballs spring up on the lawn. The shelflike polypores reach maturity and cover stumps and dead snags. But the morels, perhaps the most sought after of all, come up in the spring.

A cluster of them pushed up their spongy heads here amid a thick bed of mayapples. Only two of them were well developed, with stalks of an inch or more. Bits of the earth they had pushed through still clung to them. Most were just emerging from the leaf mold, with only their dark brownish crowns showing. The yellowish brown of the mature specimens identified them as yellow morels.

Another fungus flourished on a nearby stump. The corky shelfs of a polyporus, present the year round, formed concentric whirls of tan, brown, red, and green. Some naturalists call them "turkey tails."

The presence of these fungi brought to mind one who devoted a lifetime to the study of Maryland fungi. Coincidentally, she had lived but a few miles from this very spot. Mary E. Banning was born on April 6, 1822, near the mouth of Plaindealing Creek near Royal Oak in Talbot

County. Little is known of her early days, but she must have been fascinated by the natural beauty around her Chesapeake home. She wrote later, "From early childhood 'Toad Stools,' so called, have claimed my admiration. I was deeply impressed by their mystery and their beauty—perfectly at home in their varied forms and structure long before I had books to teach me classification."

This quotation is from the manuscript that accompanied Banning's compilation of 175 watercolor paintings, entitled "The Fungi of Maryland." This, her life's work, was never published and lay forgotten in a museum drawer in Albany, New York, for more than eighty years.

Banning had given the manuscript to Dr. Charles H. Peck, the state botanist of New York, in gratitude for the help and encouragement he offered. Though the two never met, they corresponded regularly, and Dr. Peck identified specimens sent to him. He published descriptions of sixteen of her fungi in the Museum's Annual Report in 1891.

Banning's letters reveal a person well educated and with an exceptional ability to express herself. And though she was not trained as an artist, her paintings show intricate detail and depth of color. In them we see the joy and enthusiasm she took in her mycological studies. But, other than Dr. Peck, the world of science took little interest in Mary Banning's work. Her later life was spent alone and in obscurity, until her death in a Winchester, Virginia, boarding house in 1903.

Her life and work would have remained unknown had not an unpublished biography of her been discovered in the archives of the Natural History Society of Maryland. That discovery led to the resurrection of her manuscript and to exhibitions of her paintings. Two of her finest paintings illustrate the morel and the polypore, which still flourish only a few miles from her birthplace. She has written in a careful hand under the painting of the morel: "In 1875 this plant was plentiful in one locality in Druid Hill Park (in Baltimore). Some epicure found the spot and it was exterminated in two days, never having appeared there since."

APRIL 23

Dragon Run, by canoe

The Piankatank winds its long and narrow way between two larger rivers, the York and the Tappahannock. It finds its source in the wilds of Dragon Swamp, through which meanders Dragon Run. In its upper reaches, the stream flows clear and swift, one of the least disturbed of all the Chesapeake's tributaries.

The Piankatank plays a hallowed role, though one still cloaked in mystery, in the annals of Chesapeake natural history. On its banks lived the colonial botanist John Clayton and his wife, Elizabeth. Though he held the post of Clerk of the County Court for Gloucester County from 1720 through 1773, the exact location of his estate, Windsor, is at present unknown. Two plants, the spring beauty and the interrupted fern, have been given the name Claytonia, after him. (See also the earlier entry for April 17.)

At midmorning today, more than two centuries later, the swampy floodplains along the river were pastelled with the pale green of yet another spring. Woods that had yesterday been empty and silent today were abuzz with bird song, full of sound and movement. Overnight, hordes of migrants had arrived.

For small birds, which must carefully budget their time and energy in a journey spanning two hemispheres, the Chesapeake offers a friendly haven. Food is plentiful; there are no mountains or deserts to cross and it is oriented in a north-south direction, an aid to navigation.

Some species were merely passing through: yellow-rumped warblers, headed for the spruce forests of New England, and the tail-wagging, rusty-crowned palm warblers, en route to northern Canada. Others among them will stay and make this their summer home: the prothonotary and hooded warblers and two vireos, the red-eyed and the white-eyed. All were noisy and active.

Most evident were the prothonotaries. Their ringing monotone sounded around every bend. The males, satiny orange yellow with bluish overtones in wings and tail, had arrived before the females and were frantically staking out territories. Many were exploring cavities and hollow stubs as possible nesting sites, some of which had already been claimed by chickadees. A number of conflicts resulted.

Harder to find were the hooded warblers, despite their bright plumage and sharp, staccato whistle. Retiring to the shrubby undergrowth, they kept hidden their bright lemon underparts and the jet black encircling their throats and crowns. One male posed briefly in a patch of bright sunlight.

Farther downstream, where spatterdock leaves dappled the swampy backwaters, two pairs of wood ducks leapt to the air. The females shrieked in protest as they flew off. Painted turtles, just out of hibernation and basking in their first sunshine in months, dropped off a log into the coffee-colored water. Roiling water here and a glint of bronze indicated spawning fish of some kind.

At a sharp bend, the stream flowed against sloping banks on one shore; the other was lost in a maze of flooded cypress, river birch, and sweet gum. From above, on this higher ground, the sound of falling bark betrayed the heavily spotted, rounded wings of a barred owl as it launched from a broken stub. Before vanishing, ghostlike, into the shadows, it came to rest briefly on a slim birch limb slanted across a bayou.

The owl and the birch formed a pleasing composition. The patterns and textures of the papery bark of the river birch range through the loveliest of pinkish brown tints. And, forking from the base, its trunks leaned in complementary curves.

Still farther downstream, several hundred yards from the main course of the river, a great blue heron peered

from her nest of sticks, set in the crown of a pine. She was alone; no other nest was in sight. Although great blue herons are normally communal during the breeding period, this pair preferred the solitude of Dragon Run.

APRIL 24

Rhode River

The afternoon had paled into a tranquil, cloud-free sundown. In that strange, shadowless light that follows sunset, the Bay lay still, barely distinguishable from the sky above it. The distant shoreline hung suspended on the horizon, and nearer islands floated above ghostly reflections.

A company of gulls was tracing gentle curves against the sky. Their delicate, dovelike shapes marked them as Bonaparte's, pausing here on their journey to northwestern Canada. Always delicate of manner, they rose in pliant, airy flight, then fell close to the water before rising again. Twice they repeated this almost choreographed maneuver, an aerial ballet.

First noted circling quite high over the river, they were coursing in tight, even curves. Abruptly, they closed formation, much as shorebirds do, and flew directly and swiftly toward the Bay. Then suddenly they spiraled upward, in unison, and began that strange ceremonial. Resuming the circular pattern, the gulls tightened up and repeated the rapid descent. Just before dropping, they fell into a funnel-shaped formation, like swifts coming to roost in a chimney.

A lone ring-billed gull, larger and bulkier, blundered in among them, as if in an attempt to join the party. But it floundered behind as, once more, the smaller gulls rose against the sky, wheeling and darting, dipping and crossing. And again they funneled down to the water. This time their maneuvers included some "side-slipping," turning the body sideways to lose altitude quickly, the way geese often do—but executed here with far more subtlety and finesse.

The birds were not feeding, pursuing insects in flight. Nor were they purposely moving from one place to another. Rather the performance seemed pure exhilaration, some ritual known only to the avian brain. Possibly it had to do with the approach of nightfall as the birds prepared to roost on the water.

The day ended with robin song filling the woods. And the first ovenbird of the spring delivered its emphatic crescendo, then quieted as if embarrassed by its own bravado. Finally, a whippoorwill called as river, trees, and sky became one in the darkness.

APRIL 28

Jug Bay Wetlands Center

The fresh marshes at this season are distinctly two-toned. The emerald green of new growth stands in vivid contrast to winter-withered tans and browns. As yet there is no hint of the rich color and texture that will tapestry these wetlands when spring turns to summer.

This demarcation is most striking at low tide. Exposed are the greening stems, spathes, and sprouts just emerging. Grasses and sedges still pale and sere above water are tinged with green at the base. Cattails, arum, and spatterdock, all perennials, have developed most. Established growths of cattail, with quantities of starch stored in the rhizome, have sent up new shoots from the nodes and fresh spears are already a foot high. The leaves of arum and spatterdock are now fully developed.

The seedlings of wild rice, an annual, are only six inches high, having just germinated a few weeks ago. Now strong enough to stand without the support of water, they look like corn sprouting in a field. Most of them have grown three leaves.

Every year the rice emerges in a different pattern. One spring may find it thick farther upstream than in the past. In another it may be sparse or absent where once the growth was heavy. The fragile seeds (those the birds don't find) are at the mercy of winds, tides, and currents. And, shallow-rooted, they may wash away even after germination.

The strict dichotomy of color is not as noticeable in the woodlands bordering the marsh. There, trees and shrubs just now coming to flower weave a mosaic of pale reds and siennas into the the greens of spring.

A beechwood on the riverbank lifts masses of pale, vaporous green washed with tan. The leaves are unfolding just as the trees come into flower. The winter buds are lengthening, bursting from their brownish scalelike covering and spreading their pleats. The staminate flowers aggregate into hairy clusters, pendant on frail, curving stems. Some are distinguishable as individual flowers, showing the pale olive green of the anthers. At the lightest touch, puffs of pollen waft off in the breeze.

The steep banks below the beeches are dappled with the pink of flowering azalea. The color is pure, unmarked, without the variation and venation that streaks the petals of most reddish flowers. The long, spidery stamens, curving upward, are a brighter crimson.

APRIL 29

Rhode River

Across the marshes, a faint purple glows against the dark shore. At close range, the haze resolves into starry clusters of rose magenta, the flowers of the redbud. Clinging to the smallest branches and even to the trunk itself, the flowers cover the bare slate gray limbs like strings of Christmas tree lights. Poised at the end of a curving stem, each shows the upright petals between the longer "wings" typical of the pea family. The bell-like calyx, flared like a french horn, is a darker maroon color. A few tiny leaves are unfolding, soft as velvet, yellow green with a reddish tinge.

But at close range the redbud loses the modest delicacy it shows from afar. More impressive is the effect of an entire tree, decked with magenta, tucked away in a wooded cove. A grove of wiry old redbuds stands alongside Sheepshead Cove, just off Rhode River. The tallest reach to forty feet or more and seem to be at life's end; many of the upper branches have already died. But lower, they still bloom with the vigor of youth. The bark on these ancient trees is marked with a distinctive texture not found on the average redbud. The orange cambium shows through sharply delineated ridges and cracks.

Here, a knotty-limbed, scraggly cherry lifted its snowy branches among the redbud. Feeding among the blossoms was the spring's first orchard oriole. Balancing acrobatically on the tip of a branch, it twisted its head and body at strained angles to reach into the blossoms. Hanging upside down like a chickadee, its chestnut and black

plumage showed to good advantage. It was not feeding on the petals themselves, as some birds do, but searching for insects within the corolla. It paused every few seconds to give its lively, lilting warble, paying no attention to the bees swarming around it.

Back home again, after a winter in the tropics (most of them go to South America) the oriole will stay to nest along the Chesapeake. But it will not tarry. Shortly after the young are on the wing, these orioles grow restless. By August, most of them will have returned to winter quarters, making the dangerous flight over the Gulf of Mexico.

The orchard oriole is more frequent in the Bay area than its more famous, brighter-colored cousin named after Lord Baltimore. The nesting ranges of the two species merge just north of the Chesapeake.

MAY 3

Susquehanna State Park

Relics from the Carboniferous Period have thrust anachronistic heads from the abandoned railroad bed here. The sporecaps of the field horsetail, flesh pink and thimble-shaped, have appeared as if from another age.

Some are just emerging. Others have grown to six inches or more, with soft yellowish brown sporeheads, like catkins. From the ripest, clouds of gray green spores fall away in the breeze. Along the flesh-colored stem, yellow sheathes flare up at regular intervals.

These spore-bearing growths will soon wither. Then the green fronds will spring from the rootstock, reaching heights of a foot or two and lasting through the summer. These green shoots, sometimes called scouring rushes, are miniature replicas and close relatives of the giant tree ferns we know today only from fossils.

MAY 8

Pennington Pond

Few Chesapeake fishermen respect the carp. To most, this sluggish bottom-feeder does little more than muddy the water and clog nets and traps. A few find it a challenging target when hunting with bow and arrow. But in Europe it is considered a worthy adversary, valiant when hooked. Izaak Walton himself called it the "Queen of Rivers." It is worshipped in Asia, its native home, where it is honored with festivals and religious ceremonies. In

Japan, the Carp Festival, *Koi Noburi*, is held annually on May 5. This celebration must coincide with the spawning season there; it is about then that Chesapeake waters warm sufficiently for carp to spawn.

Carp hereabouts are transformed during the first weeks of May from drowsy, slow-moving fish to frenzied, powerful swimmers. In piscine ecstasy, several gathered today in the shallow water at the head of the pond, chasing, wallowing, and wriggling. The water, barely deep enough for them to swim, became liquid mud amid the thrashing tails and swirling bodies. Fertilization must depend wholly on

chance; in that melee, sex recognition could hardly have been possible.

Carp, incidentally, were first introduced into this country at Druid Hill Park in Baltimore in 1877. Placed in ponds prepared for them, they were brought from Germany by a representative of the U.S. Fish Commission. From this original stock, they were distributed to suitable waters throughout the country.

MAY 9

Rhode River

An ancient black walnut tree anchoring a bit of the shoreline stood, a solitary sentinel above the cove and an open meadow. Centuries old, its dead upper limbs reached skeletal fingers into the sky. Eddying gusts of swallows whirled above these topmost branches, then settled among them, gathering side by side, occupying every available niche.

They had hardly come to rest when they all flew, en masse, out over the water, lifting and veering in unison. Just as abruptly they returned, scrambling for positions they had moments ago vacated. Swarming in wild, festive abandon and assuming all manner of twists and postures, their actions were anxious, hurried. The reckless sorties over the water continued. Once they mounted high, then descended, like wind blown smoke, in a sort of funneling motion. It was late in the day, and this extraordinary behavior could well have been some sort of preroosting ritual.

Among the hundreds of tree swallows were a small number of barn swallows and a single, lost female purple martin. All were apparently preparing to spend the night in the old walnut.

It was quite dark when, from the deep shadows under the bank, sounded the clear, sharp "peet-weet" of a spotted sandpiper. From an island across the water, another answered. From yet another quarter, farther off, drifted the same wistful plaint. Then the nearest one called again. For several minutes these melancholy strains echoed over the darkening expanse:

fragments of life seeking contact with others of their kind.

MAY 10

Black Swamp Creek

In Bay country, great blue herons gather to nest on islands or in remote swamps. Few of these sites are accessible without a boat, and, once reached, their bulky stick nests are normally so high off the ground that little can be seen of them. An exception is the colony at Black Swamp Creek.

There, from a hillside above, one can actually look down on the nesting herons, so their home life can be studied with relative ease and little disturbance to the nesting birds. On lands administered by the Department of Natural Resources, the colony is monitored and protected. Some hundred nests crowd the upper branches of two large sycamores, sequestered at the head of the marsh-lined creek. Because foliage on these trees was still in the budding stage, there was little to obstruct the view. Within a week, all would be hidden among the new leaves.

The birds, unnerved at first, soon settled down to family matters. Parent herons arrived steadily from the direc-

tion of the river, coasting in on wide, rounded wings, gangling limbs grasping for position. The larger youngsters lunged forward to be fed, so eager they seemed to be in danger of falling to the ground. Other nestlings, not so well grown, lay prone, barely lifting their heads. Most nests sheltered two young; in several there were four.

Many of the offspring were about the size of their parents, though sporting the paler, more spotted juvenal plumage. Clownish-looking spikes of down still adorned their crowns. Others half this size squatted, their legs folded under them. These younger birds showed more dark in the head, especially about the eye, and were tinged with maroon on the breast. The wings were little more than pinfeathers. The youngest hatchlings, completely clad in natal down, were a smoky gray, paling to white on their sides and back. Erect masses of down gave them a comic, bushy aspect.

Sensing at once the approach of the adults, the young opened their bills and clamored for food. But upon arrival, the old birds usually spent a moment or two in quiet dignity, long necks alertly erect, before feeding.

Deal Island

A monster snapping turtle, its head the size of a baseball, blocked a sandy road. I would have thought it the granddaddy of all snapping turtles, except that it was a mama. She had apparently lumbered up from the marsh to lay her eggs in the soft mud of a drying puddle.

Though the middle of a road was obviously a poor choice for a nesting site, she did not intend to change her mind. She raised herself menacingly on fleshy, flabby legs covered with warty scales. A hissing, like escaping steam, issued from within her gaping, hooked jaws. She seemed stuffed into a shell ridiculously small for her girth. Her bulging sides and underparts were exposed, her legs and feet too large to be retracted. These barrel-shaped appendages lifted the creature a full two inches above the ground.

Folds of loose flesh encircled the neck, from which extended the massive head. A thick, muscular tail was armored with a formidable row of toothlike knobs. Three distinct ridges marked a carapace coated with mud and draped with decayed vegetable matter. The turtle's eyes, placed high toward the front of the head, could be

looked into from directly above. The pupil was black, faintly ringed with pale gold, the iris a muddy gray with lighter radiations like the spokes of a wagon wheel.

She wanted only to get on with her egg laying. Though she had not yet begun to dig a nest, beneath her hind legs were the initial scrapings of an excavation. Tracks on the road showed that she had wandered more than a hundred yards in search of a spot that suited her. So I left her there to fulfill her instincts for procreation, despite the uncertain future of her progeny.

MAY 16

Choptank River at Dover Bridge

A morning fog had not quite dissolved by midday, but the sun shone through, drenching the wide marshes here with luminous yellow. Every blade and stem shimmered with reflecting moisture, sending out millions of points of light. The tallest panicles glistened as if touched with frost. Across the marsh, even through this golden haze, springtime green contrasted with the withered old growth.

New stands of arum, two feet

high, had already developed large, full-sized arrow-shaped leaves. The slender flowering spathes were just emerging. Other tufts of bright green dappled the shallow water. The most extensive were topped with purplish blue, the flowers of the blue flag, our largest

native iris. A luxuriant clump close by the road allowed careful study of the intricate flowers.

Delicately symmetrical, the flowers were a symphony of threes, a triad of radiating sets of threes. On the outside of the perianth, the sepals, petal-like in color and texture, reached upward and fell in graceful, spatulate curves. Each of these had a yellow blaze at its base. The shorter inner segments, the true petals, stood upright. The style in the center, with its three wide branches, gave the appearance of yet three more petals. These branches arched closely over and hid the three stamens. The pale blues were veined and striated with darker blues and hints of yellow.

These blues reflected in the tidal pools and narrow guts that sauntered off back into the marsh. Beyond, over the main channel of the river, birds coursed by, most of them moving steadily to the north. Those on passage found the open water a convenient flyway.

A flock of shorebirds, too small and distant to identify, whirled over, then changed course and eventually settled on the exposed mud. Restless, they had just begun to feed when a lone yellowlegs yelped a warning and all were up and off again. These little

"peep," as they are known collectively, still had half a continent ahead of them. They must reach Arctic breeding grounds by early June if they are to complete the nesting cycle during the short northern summer.

From the sky to the east, beyond newly plowed fields, drifted the wind-blown cry of another world traveler: the black-bellied plover. Scores of these handsome waders, forsaking their normal seashore haunts, were feeding among the freshly turned clods. They were also bound for Arctic slopes, and the vagaries of wind and weather had brought them inland, where they had paused to rest and refuel. A few were still in gray winter livery, the majority in crisp black and white.

While the shorebirds still had a long flight ahead of them, many of the local birds had already nested. Three species had selected cavity homes in a scrubby, half-dead willow hanging over the riverbank. Woodpecker excavations had provided living quarters for two pairs of tree swallows, a family of house wrens, and a nestful of noisy starlings. An apartment complex!

Only the starlings appeared to have young. Two nestlings, about ready to leave home, wrestled for space at the entrance hole. The wrens fussed and fumed at my nearness, but the swallows fearlessly hovered and fluttered about, going in and out of their nest holes.

MAY 18

Pennington Pond

It is not only migrating water birds that use the Bay as a flyway, as a navigational aid. Songbirds and raptors follow its shorelines as well and use the north-south orientation of the Chesapeake as a landmark. Daytime migrants such as hawks, jays, and swallows tend to concentrate at key locations along the water's course. Birds that fly at night follow the same pattern, but are, of course, less noticeable. An exceptionally strong flight last evening, coincidental with a changing weather system, offered telling evidence of such a nocturnal passage.

For reasons not clearly understood, most small birds migrate at night. Why should so many species, normally diurnal in their habits, prefer to fly after dark? It may have to do with safety from predation or, as one theory holds, because they use the stars to maintain a course. Possibly the night air, cooler and more humid, is more favorable to flight. And night fliers have the entire day to feed, a further advantage.

Two hours after sunset, at about half past ten, bird sound filled the darkness overhead. For a full hour their calls rained down: thrushes, warblers, tanagers, and grosbeaks. Some gave loud, metallic "chip" notes; others whistled softly or barely lisped. All seemed to be flying much lower than normal, judging from the nearness of their calls. And there seemed an anxiety, an urgency in their voices.

The cause for such apprehension was an approaching weather front. An overcast associated with the front had veiled the stars, and the wind had moved sharply from the south around to the northwest, directly confronting the birds. Moreover, precipitation approached from the north. Such adverse conditions resulted in what ornithologists call a "fall-out," or simply a "fall." Disoriented and confused, the birds were finally forced to the ground in unusual concentrations. As a result, the woods this morning were swarming with migrants. An effervescence of bird song continued without a break. The treetops stirred with their fuss and fidget.

Most prominent were the yellow-rumped warblers, dapper in black

and white with smudges of bright
yellow. One crisply tailored male was
busily ferreting out insects or larvae
from drooping clumps of oak catkins.
It took time, every thirty seconds or
so, to lift its head in song: a sibilant
whisper that grew louder as one note
tumbled into another. Black and white

warblers, zebras of the bird world, crept mouselike around tree trunks. They sang less frequently and with little conviction.

Keeping to the higher branches was a parula warbler, revealing only its yellow throat and breast, broken with a rainbow of maroon and burnt orange. Its buzzy trill went up the scale, then fell over the top. From lower down in the understory erupted the musical chatter of a Canada warbler, a dark necklace across its lemon breast. Yellowish "spectacles" gave it an odd, wide-eyed look. Also flitting low were redstarts, two coquettish females in blue gray with yellow in their wings and tails, and then the male, coal black with fiery embers in his half-opened wings and tail.

Never had I seen such a collection of wood warblers, each jewel-like in the intensity of its color. Two others showed themselves, a tiger-striped magnolia and the Blackburnian, whose throat does seem to be afire (though its name derives not from its brilliant plumage but from a certain Mr. Blackburn.) Its song, weak and high-pitched, was delivered from the tip of a swaying branch, offering a rare, unobstructed view.

But topping them all was a gem I could not at first identify. Its song hinted at the Blackburnian's: very high and so faint as to be barely audible. But it was tantalizingly different, and the little rascal would not show itself. For ten frustrating minutes I caught nothing but a flutter of leaves here, a flitting shadow there. Finally, my neck stiffened from craning at the canopy, I managed a glimpse of its head: ebony cheeks, inlaid with glowing mahogany in the crown and throat and along the sides. A bay-breasted warbler! Once it had let itself be known, it gave in, dropping to a lower branch and singing fearlessly in full sight, a visual delight that was enhanced by the knowledge that this feathered mite was bound from Colombia in South America to the spruce forests of northern Canada.

Yet other riches lurked in the newborn foliage. A rose-breasted grosbeak, stark black and white with a blood red triangle across its front, delivered its bell-clear song, each phrase slurring into the next. Similar, but more hoarse, were the notes of a scarlet tanager, which glowed tropically red.

Vireos, flycatchers, and thrushes added to the list, each with its own nuances of color and voice. Here, only because of a forced interruption, they will feed and rest, then be on their way. Tomorrow may find them hundreds of miles distant.

Kings Landing County Park

An overcast afternoon with moisture heavy in the air stimulated an early chorus of spring peepers. It

began shortly after four, with the first hesitant chirp. Scattered pipings answered, and soon there were dozens of mingled voices, the chant growing louder. Individually, the tiny frog voice rings frail, feeble. But collectively! The clamor!

Above this shrill crescendo resonated a slow, vibrant trill. Twice it sounded, a toadlike purr. Then again, from a different location. I could not trace the source of the sound, which I recognized as the call of the gray tree frog. Strangely ventriloquistic and masterfully camouflaged, the creature could well have been within a few feet, or it might have been hidden in a cavity or woodpecker hole.

Though I have often heard them, it was quite by accident that I finally saw a gray tree frog. As I grasped the trunk of a sapling to balance myself while crossing a stream, I felt a soft, puttylike wad against my hand. Despite such a startling intrusion, this phlegmatic individual remained, adhering as if plastered to the limb. Fat and squat, it was about two inches long with wrinkled, warty skin. The blunt head was nearly shapeless, the eyes large and bulging. Its toes extended into broad, rounded discs. The mottled, grayish brown skin was remarkably like the color and texture of bark.

An extended leg showed a splash of orange yellow.

On another occasion I discovered one, again quite by accident, resting atop a fence post. Its feet were folded under its body, which was pressed tightly against the post, completely obscuring its outline and rendering it barely discernible.

Especially captivating was another tree frog, captured and kept briefly in a terrarium at the Jug Bay Estuarine Park on the Patuxent River. Calm and trusting, it seemed at home, calling in response to the electronic buzzing of the telephone.

MAY 23

Sellman Creek

The red fox is known for its wily cunning, for its ingenuity in hiding and escaping from humankind. So I was surprised to find an active den in the middle of an open grassy slope just above an old farm road. A mound of light colored earth before the entrance made it even more conspicuous.

Three cubs watched, more in curiosity than in alarm, when I stopped the car for a better look. As I opened the door they retreated to the burrow but remained in sight until

I walked toward them. Carcasses and bones were scattered about the opening. The legs and tail of a woodchuck, still attached to the skin, were recognizable, as were the feathers of a blackbird and a flicker. Bits of fur strewn about could have come from a cottontail rabbit.

A few yards higher and around the curve of the hillside, a mound of sandy earth marked another den—or perhaps a back entrance to the same one. As I walked toward it, a shrill yapping sounded from the wood's edge. There sat an adult fox on its haunches. She (I supposed it was the vixen) barked again, in apparent concern for her young, possibly as a warning to them. She managed to bark while holding something in her jaws. While I watched, she vanished into the scrubby woods as if into thin air. I did not catch any movement; one moment she was there, in the next she was gone.

The den was less than half a mile from where I had seen a fox trot across the frozen creek in the gloom of a February dusk; from where I had also heard the eerie, catlike screaming of mating foxes.

Nassawango Creek, by canoe

The Pocomoke River has its source in the cypress swamps just north of the Maryland-Delaware line. It flows southward for some thirty miles, through forested bottom land, before it enters into Pocomoke Sound, where it is bordered by wide sweeps of salt marsh. Fourteen miles farther it empties into Chesapeake Bay. Throughout its length, the total fall of the river is less than thirty feet.

Such poor drainage accounts for the sluggish flow of the stream and for the swampy, flooded lands that border its shores. These swamps extend from one-half to two miles inland. Much of this low country is subject to tidal inundation, with a daily rise and fall of two to three feet.

Once an impenetrable haven for smugglers, bootleggers, and runaway slaves, the Pocomoke forest was long ago exploited for its timber, and parts of the original swamp were cleared and drained for agriculture. But much of it remains undisturbed, forming one of the wildest, least altered areas in the entire Chesapeake watershed.

A vital portion of the swamp has come under the protection of the Nature Conservancy. Through this tract meanders Nassawango Creek, its nineteen miles forming the largest tributary of the Pocomoke. At its mouth is an extensive fresh marsh, and its upper reaches have much surface vegetation. Since the land barely rises along its banks, there is only a gradual transition from river to swamp to upland forest.

Today, a lush fullness of foliage and flower lay along its shores in the late afternoon sun, rendering the aspect

more like summer than spring. Huge, buttressed cypresses stood along the banks, their feathery leaves a pale green. Isolated cypress knees emerged, like the humped backs of underwater creatures. Ash and gum trees towered beyond, their reflections darkening the water. In the understory, shrubs and smaller trees were heavy with blossom. Blanketing the shallower stretches of water were the broad leaves of the yellow pond lily or spatterdock.

The globular flowers of the pond lily, in various stages of growth, arched above the tide. Some were in full bloom, others were in bud, and a few had already faded. These odd-looking flowers are marvels of intricate design and function. The conspicuous yellow sepals form a cup, inside of which are the petals, tinged a delicate pink and so small and numerous they resemble scales. From the center radiate the numerous stamens and pistils, the whole comprising a pattern of remarkable symmetry. When the flower first opens, the undeveloped stamens remain hidden, thus insuring cross-fertilization.

In places the creek merely wandered off into the forest or into coves and inlets leading nowhere. Where there was a distinct shoreline, thick, shrubby growth covered the banks.

The dark green there was bedecked with whitish blossoms: elderberry, viburnum, sweet bay, and tassel-white, or sweet spires.

The elderberry formed heavy thickets, the flat-topped umbels reaching ten to twelve feet above the water. The bunched flowers resembled flecks of foam, washed somehow to the tips of branches. Similar inflorescences of the arrowwood viburnum were lower, just above the water.

Here also, near the northern limit of its range, was the tassel-white, or sweet-spires. Its minute flowers, with five star-shaped petals, climbed curving racemes. Even tinier were the short-stalked blossoms of the winterberry holly. Clinging close to the twig and barely noticeable at this season, they will ripen into bright red fruits come September.

Largest and most conspicuous were the flowers of the sweet bay, or swamp magnolia. The showy petals, two to three inches across, were set among sprays of smooth, shiny leaves. Only a few flowers graced each tree, but they filled the air with fragrance and will continue to bloom through a six-week period.

The red bay, a distant relative of this magnolia, also reaches its northern limit in the Pocomoke swamps. It was first found there in 1809 by the naturalist-explorer Thomas Nuttall, on his first major collecting trip after having crossed the Atlantic from his native England. In June of that year he traveled on foot through the cypress swamps near Dagsbury (now Dagsboro) in Delaware. (The red bay was not found again in Delaware until 130 years later.) After leaving Dagsboro, Nuttall journeyed to the headwaters of the Nanticoke River, which was the extent of his excursion into Chesapeake Country (though years later he did sail down the Potomac).

As the creek snaked deep into the swamp, in endless, labyrinthine twists, it flowed past stands of wild iris, the blue flags. In large, compact clumps, these were the slender blue flags that come to flower later than their larger relative, which earlier had brightened the more open meadows and marshes.

The most plentiful of the birds in the swamp was perhaps its most attractive: the prothonotary warbler, flashing golden yellow. The males, like those noted six weeks earlier at Dragon Run, were investigating every hollow and cavity they came to. One peeped out from the large opening of a nesting box erected for wood ducks.

The wood duck hen had already hatched her brood. Nearby she was leading them across a patch of open water. Sensing danger at the approach of the canoe, she uttered a low "kuk," sending the young into a wild scramble for cover. They splashed into the bankside foliage while their mother flew off upstream, hurtling acrobatically through overhanging branches. A thorough search of the spot where the youngsters disappeared turned up nothing.

Farther upstream, anxious, excited cries echoed around a bend. A pair of red-shouldered hawks had been aroused by some intruder or another. A half dozen crows arrived to see what all the fuss was about. They quieted, then fled at the approach of the canoe. In a nest lodged in the lowest crotch of a cypress, only fifteen feet above the stream, was the probable cause of all the fuss: two young hawks, still in downy white.

Later, as the rays of the setting sun slanted through the trees, a wood thrush sang, clear and mellow. And from atop a loblolly a yellow-throated warbler intoned, a sweet chattering falling off at the end.

In the twilight, a bullfrog pronounced ownership of a plant-choked backwater. Across the stream another bellowed. The large head of yet one more projected above the water, disappeared, then reappeared closer. Was this a female, attracted to the call?

JUNE 12

Barren Island

Blustery showers had moved through during the night, and at dawn a dark bank of cloud clung to the horizon, so dense that it appeared as a distant range of mountains. Above, a new day shaded upward, through lemon yellow to the palest of blues. The sunrise flushed with salmon pink the sandy flats that crept out from the island. White birds resting on the beach and in flight were washed with the same hue.

All were terns, greyhound-slim and silvery-winged. Those in the air wheeled about in a confused tangle,

skirmishing and chasing, their voices shrill and raucous. When they dropped to the sand they were immediately subject to attack. Every cry or gesture from one bird evoked a response from another nearby. All of this furious maneuvering, of chase and escape, was actually a process of getting together. It was a time for pairing off, for mating, and thus a time of tension and conflict. Apparently, there were differences to be resolved before happy partnerships could be formed. Even pairs already mated were restlessly displaying and posturing.

Fish were a vital part of the ritual. A tern arriving with a fish in its bill immediately excited three or four others, and the chase was on. One such "fish flight" lasted ten minutes, with much diving and evasive action over the water.

One tern dropped lightly to the beach, a four-inch fish gleaming in its bill. With stiff, mincing gait, it walked toward another tern and nudged it with its breast, all the while chattering with excitement. Lifting its wings vertically above its back, it offered the fish. She (now obviously the female of the pair) paid no attention to the fish, but crouched low in a submissive attitude. Just then another tern abruptly intervened, alighting next to them with a smaller fish. In an instant, still another dived directly into their midst, screaming wildly. All four then dashed off together.

Within a minute, the original pair (I think) returned. The male paraded around his intended, fluttering his wings and patting his feet rapidly. He trod around and around, kneading his feet rapidly, but evoked no response from the female. He still offered the fish, which she continued to ignore.

After a few moments of awkward ceremony, the fish dangling between them, came the fulfillment. The male assumed an odd, stilted posture, his forked tail raised, head held high, wings half open. She crouched before him and they copulated. She then took the fish and flew away.

Subtle differences marked most of the birds as Forster's terns. Smaller numbers of common terns showed darker primaries and deeper red bills. Clumsy and ungainly in comparison were a dozen or so herring gulls, mere bystanders, that loafed on a delta of sand.

The ternery itself was not on this stretch of beach. The nests were woven among grasses on a tiny islet south of the main island. Hardly an acre in extent, its cover was mostly of

spartina grass, with smaller stands of three-square sedge. Sea rocket was coming into bloom on the bare, sandy edges. A shrubby growth of marsh elder was the only woody vegetation where a narrow gut curled out from an open pool near the islet's center.

Later, with the tide running full, we were able to push ashore there. In dizzying confusion, the birds rose at once, circling and crossing, rising and falling. Several terns darted at our heads, shrieking in protest. Among a hundred or so terns were a dozen dark-headed laughing gulls.

Little effort was made to conceal the nests, which were scattered about the whole island. Saucer-shaped cups of woven grass, they were placed atop piles of dead grass and tidal wrack. They were but a few feet apart in some instances. Carefully and skillfully constructed, they were lined with smaller, finer grasses. In each hollow were three or four eggs, buff ochre with dark chocolate scrawling. Slightly larger eggs with a lighter ground color belonged to the laughing gull. Built on a higher platform of grasses, the gull nests were of sturdier construction and furnished a deeper cradle for the eggs.

Several nests housed newly hatched tern chicks, their down still wet. As cryptically colored as the eggs they came from, their little bodies were dabbed and patched with dark, resembling bits of debris on a beach. Naked pinfeathers covered the stumps that will be wings. Remarkably, even at that age they made feeble efforts to scramble for cover.

I did not want to keep the parents too long away from their nests. The eggs were vulnerable, as were the newborn chicks, to the killing heat of the sun. So after a few minutes I left, to investigate what was left of the biggest island. Through the years, it had eroded badly. Within the memory of a generation, it had been 700 acres or more in size and had supported a thriving community with stores, a church, and several farms. The last families left in 1916, floating their houses across Tar Bay to Hooper's Island. The Bay is now claiming the last building there, a hunting lodge. Half of it has disappeared, the remainder toppling lopsidedly. Ospreys had piled nesting material onto the roof.

A pine forest still thrived at one end of the island. Within it was a nesting colony of great blue herons. Most of the nests were hidden in the foliage, but gangly youngsters could be seen atop two of them. Peering from the crowns of the pines, adult birds

watched with some concern. Other herons cruised back and forth from the mainland.

Two bald eagles, dark immature birds, lifted from the marshy borders of a beachside pond. One flew to a bulky nest in an isolated pine. They had perhaps just fledged, and still had a strong attachment to their home-place.

A mile or so to the north, narrow white strands caught the sun. All that is left of a series of islands, these beaches supported very little vegeta-tion but did provide the few feet of ground high enough for herring gulls to nest. Of the fifteen nests there, five sheltered chicks large enough to tod-dle off. Mere scrapes in the sand, with rootlets and flotsam pushed around

passage of migratory birds, no awakening from a winter's sleep, no unfolding of leaf heralds the summer season. There is not then the resurrection, the burgeoning of life that marks the coming of spring.

Summer here is a gentle fruition, the gradual attainment of promises made in spring. And in these latitudes, the fulfillment of such pledges does not wait for the solstice, for a specific day of the year. It is summer when the marshes are shoulder-high, when cattail spikes spill golden pollen, when the redwings bring off their first nestlings.

So, although officially it was still spring, it was summerlike as I slid the canoe in among the waterside reeds. The river lay still in the pallid light preceding the sunrise, and thin mists hung in the warming air. Wooded islands offshore, a leafy green at midday, now stood gray. When the sky lightened to peach yellow, it glowed through the mists and reflected in pools between tussocks of grass, where a heron stalked.

Over the water, barn swallows swept back and forth in endless gyrations. These were family gatherings, the juvenile swallows having just fledged from nests under a nearby pier. Still under the care of their par-

them, the others contained two eggs each. A moderately high tide could have washed them all away.

JUNE 13

Tuckahoe Creek, by canoe

In Chesapeake country, spring merges seamlessly with summer. No

ents, a trio of these youngsters clung uneasily to the curving stems of reed grass, where they waited to be fed. Much chatter and flutter greeted the adults when they brought food, which they delivered in flight.

Other swallows settled at the muddy edges of a roadside pool of rain, where they collected bits of moist earth. In their bills were tiny strands of grass, used with mud to attach their nests to the pier supports. Hardly had they raised one brood than they were already building anew in preparation for another.

Among the swallows whirled two others, more robust in profile and lacking the barn swallow's forked tail. One of these rough-winged swallows swooped to perch on an exposed root dangling from the bankside. Just below it was a cavity, most likely dug out by kingfishers. From within came the peeping of young swallows.

Offshore, an osprey nest was draped over the fallen remnants of a duck blind. Only a few feet above the water, I could look into the nest from the canoe. Crouched on the platform were four young, nearly the size of their parents, laying prone, instinctively trying to hide. Other ospreys had also prospered along the course of the stream. On channel

markers, duck blinds, and atop boathouses, wherever there was room there were nests.

Painted turtles, more alert and athletic than their terrestrial cousins, dropped into the water whenever the canoe neared their basking logs. But one that I discovered on land in a sandy clearing seemed unaccountably groggy, until I saw that she had come ashore to lay eggs. She hesitated at first, but when I did not approach closer, she resumed her digging. If I moved, even slightly, she paused for minutes at a time, her eyes narrowed to slits. When she drew the sand under herself, with her back feet turned inward, it became evident that she was not making a hole but covering one up, having already laid her eggs. She went off, stepping quickly, without fully covering the hollow.

Clumps of swamp milkweed, just coming into bloom at a marshy bend in the creek, had attracted swarms of insect visitors. The purplish red flowers, more plum-colored than those of the common milkweed, are a favored nectar source for bees and butterflies. Half a dozen tiger swallowtails fed in clusters or careened about erratically, usually returning to the same plant they had left. Two of them exhibited the dark form of the female;

both looked a bit worn and ragged and one had a missing tail. There was no sign of mating or courtship activity.

The silver-spotted skippers, also attracted to this clump of milkweed, were definitely interested in the opposite sex. In constant motion with frequent aerial encounters, they hardly paused long enough to mate. Finally, with no apparent preliminaries, a pair positioned themselves back to back, one curving its abdomen to meet that of its mate.

Keeping to itself was yet another butterfly, deep orange and rusty brown above, with a pattern of white spotting on the underwing. Longer-lived than most butterflies, this great spangled fritillary may live through the summer, even into early autumn, if it is a female. At that time she will deposit her eggs on the leaves or stems of violets. The caterpillars will emerge within days, and the fate of the species will be entrusted to these delicate larvae and their ability to endure the winter. It will be yet another spring before they emerge as butterflies and so begin the cycle from promise to fulfillment.

Bodkin Island

Forty years ago, Bodkin Island in Eastern Bay covered five acres, with nearly a mile of shoreline. A fringe of salt marsh surrounded it, and a sandy beach connected points of higher ground, where groves of loblollies stood. Beneath the pines, a hunter's cabin nestled.

But erosion was even then taking its toll. Wind and tides, abetted by storms and the wakes from boats, tore at its shorelines. By the sixties the beach had disappeared, and a hundred yards of shallow water divided the island. In the seventies, the loblollies gave way, their rooted stumps persisting and standing ten yards offshore. By then the most northerly of the island's remnants had vanished all together.

Today, Bodkin consists of less than one acre of fast ground covered with scraggly vegetation. A few scrubby pines hang on amidst a tangle of vines and saplings. Gone are its beaches and marshes. In their place, an encircling bulkhead has been erected by the state in an attempt to save what is left. So depleted, Bodkin hardly seems a suitable location for large numbers of nesting birds. But such island sites, safe from predation and human disturbance, are at a premium in this part of the Bay. Precious few places with the necessary habitat and isolation remain. And so, on this late spring day, this fragile bit of Chesapeake shore was crowded with the nests of herons and terns.

Cattle egrets, their whites softened with the tawny cinnamon of fresh breeding plumage, stood like Christmas decorations against the dark foliage. Colorful plumes flowed from their necks and backs. Young egrets, fuzzy headed and gangly, clambered clumsily over poison ivy vines. The newly hatched young, still in the nest, were protected from the midday sun by their parents. Parties of adult cattle egrets crossed to and from the mainland, flying just over the water.

Less numerous were the snowy egrets, daintier and more fluid of movement. Not upset at the intrusion, they merely scrambled to reach better vantage points, where their lacy nuptial plumes caught the breeze. Young snowies, still in natal down, huddled on twiggy platforms a few feet from the ground. Above them, a lone great egret, nervously alert, stood a neck higher than the others. A breeze lifted the lacy feathers from its back.

Against this massed whiteness, other herons were noticeably darker.

Poised on a bare stub, in full view, was a little blue, deep ultramarine overall, with tones and gradations toward purple. Even its bill was a rich blue. More subtly colored, but equally exquisite, was a tricolored heron. Its delicate blue grays, tinged with lavender, were intensified by the pure whites on the belly and neck.

Hanging about the periphery of the island, a dozen green herons looked on. They showed quiet concern for their nests and young, hidden in the undergrowth. Throughout most of their range, green herons are solitary nesters; this group preferred the safety and security of an island colony.

A narrow band of salt meadow grass, the softest of the spartinas, carpeted the sloping edge at one end of the island. From these tufts peered the heads of nesting common terns. In alert, upright positions they brooded, wings crossing in the manner of swallows over their backs. Loathe to leave the eggs, they sat tight, showing well the stark black and white of their heads and the vivid scarlet of their black-tipped bills.

Eventually, with piercing cries of protest, they rose in a swarm. Hovering directly above, they planed and hurtled downward, brushing my head with their wings. But when I withdrew they quieted immediately, spiraled down with dexterous twists of wing, and shuffled back onto the eggs. Substantial cradles of woven grass, most of the nests contained but one grayish ochre egg, scrawled and spotted with dark brown. Laying must have just started, as a full clutch normally consists of three or four.

Seven ducklings following a black duck hen scuttled in single file to the safety of the water. Offshore, the little flotilla bobbed, still close behind their mother. This brood was likely the happy result of a second nesting; most black ducklings hatch in mid-April. Indeed, fourteen nests were counted on this very island back in April.

As the family moved into open water, I wondered how long there would be an island here on which they can nest.

JUNE 15

Nanticoke River

Earlier in spring, state fishery biologists had sampled the catches of commercial fishermen here to get data on the spawning runs of the alosids, the herring and shad that move upstream to spawn in fresh water. In the course of these studies, they took

note of spawning rockfish, perch, and crappie. Today, biologists sampled the waters farther upstream in an effort to determine spawning success.

By trawling at mid-depth, at slow speeds, they could capture only this year's fry; larger fish could avoid the sweep of the net. Stations were tested at regular intervals on the Nanticoke proper and on its largest tributaries, Marshyhope and Broad Creeks. The entire circuit by boat covered a distance of seventy-two miles.

The first haul, on the Nanticoke just above Vienna, where the salinity measured two parts per thousand, netted only half a dozen alewives and a few white perch, all only a little more than inch long. Tiny menhaden, hatched in the ocean and carried up the Bay by currents and tides, were also included in the catch.

In the fresher waters of the Marshyhope, alewives were even smaller. Catfish fry, at that tender age looking a lot like tadpoles, were also brought in. Upstream, the alewives were smaller yet. The older and larger the fish, the farther they had moved downstream in the first stage of their migration to coastal waters. They remain at sea until reaching maturity, in three to six years.

Off Broad Creek, juvenile herring measured barely an inch. Here, where we had observed them spawning in April, were numerous two-inch rockfish. Earlier, in another measure to study spawning rates, Maryland Department of Natural Resource biologists had found eggs in over 80 percent of plankton net samples.

The Nanticoke and Marshyhope flow through swamps of ash and maple that grow to the shoreline. Few shallow water flats have formed where marshland can develop. But in the coves and backwaters, narrow stands of fresh marsh had found a foothold. Here, wild rice, though only half-grown, arched long arabesque curves over arrow arum and pickerelweed.

The spathes of arum, heavy with developing seed, drooped into the water. But pickerelweed was just then lifting spires of blue blossom. Clustered on racemes, each flower was about an inch across. The upper parts of the funnel-shaped petals bore two yellow spots, marks that possibly helped to guide a crowd of visiting bees to the nectar source. Though each flower of the pickerelweed blooms for only one day, the plant will continue to unfold through the summer and into October.

JUNE 16

Mayo Beach

Dense beds of vegetation, submerged at low tide, have formed along the margins of the Bay and the inlet here. A rich yellow green, they lie prostrate on the mud at low tide, but become erect, undulating with the current, when covered by water. Each is an individual plant, and once the the narrow leaves are carefully separated, the tiny capsular seeds of the horned pondweed are revealed. Slightly curved, each bears a beaklike protuberance.

Each spring growths of this pondweed, one of the earliest of the submerged plants to appear along the Chesapeake, flourishes where fresh and brackish waters mix. Its distribution varies each year, depending on the rainfall that flows from the drainage system.

A healthy growth has formed here this spring, creating a colorful background for the two snowy egrets that pranced about in this morning's sunlight, and for the great blue heron that fished with more patience, a pale statue in the yellow green shallows. Meanwhile, a muskrat crouched in dense growth, munching the narrow leaves.

JUNE 17

Poplar Island

Geologists tell us that the Chesapeake was formed eight to ten thousand years ago by the glacial melting that flooded the Susquehanna River valley. Its boundaries have been in constant flux ever since. For no two successive days has the shoreline been precisely the same. Today the Bay claims a little more land; tomorrow it may leave some.

Many islands have been completely washed away. Sharps Island, which was near the mouth of the Choptank, has disappeared, all four hundred fifty acres of it. Nearby Poplar Island is almost gone. By 1914, Poplar had already been wave-lashed into three fragments. It was then reduced to five hundred acres, from the one thousand recorded on a 1640 land deed. Today, two of the three segments, since named Jefferson Island and Coaches Island, maintain but a few acres of fast land. At high tide, the original Poplar Island is little more than a sandbar. There are plans to rebuild it, using dredge fill.

Jefferson Island was the site of the famous Democratic Club, a rendezvous and hunting lodge for politicians and statesmen. Franklin D. Roosevelt was a frequent visitor. After a fire, it was rebuilt and used as a lodge and an inn. This building still stands, precariously close to the shore.

On this warm spring day, the island was left to the birds. A bevy of terns hung over the waves, hovering and diving. Others relaxed along with three kinds of gulls on the pilings of the abandoned pier. None of them appeared to be breeding.

Eagles, however, had raised two youngsters on the island. Nearly the size of their parents, they peered from

a nest in a dead pine set within a grove of live trees. It would be several weeks before they could fly. Neither adult eagle made an appearance, but ospreys squealed in complaint from all sides.

On a grassy islet, three osprey nests, barely twenty yards apart, rested virtually on the ground. Atop platforms of tidal debris and vegetation, each cradled two full-sized youngsters. Such ground nests are only successful on small islands where there are no mammalian predators. The birds had used dead branches and driftwood, weaving into them an array of human refuse: a piece of oar, a fisherman's rubber glove, a section of door mat, a styrofoam food carton, net floats, and fishing lures.

To the west, on what little was left of Poplar Island proper, crowded more than a hundred cormorants. They barely found foothold on the few bare trees left. Each trunk, isolated and nearly shorn of branches, was crowned with a cormorant—living totem poles.

An eerie silence pervaded the place: none of the noise and bustle normally associated with a nesting colony. Most of the nests here, too, were on the ground, but the low tide did not permit a closer approach.

To the south, Coaches Island supported a dense growth of pines. Against these dark evergreens, heron nests showed as pale gray splotches. A steady stream of commuters crossed back and forth from the mainland, several miles off. From the heart of the colony emanated an odd chugging, throaty sound.

A pair of willets coursing over the marshy beach at one end of the island shrieked "Come here willy, come here willy." Earlier, one had called steadily from high above: its flight song. It took some searching to find it, hovering, wings aquiver against the clouds. Was it saluting its mate, or might it have been praising the glory of a day in June?

A cownose ray surfaced above the choppy waves offshore. Like a cross between a pancake and a shark, it ricocheted across the troughs, sliding in and out of the crests. Another appeared, slapping the water resoundingly when a wave upset the rhythm of its glide. Rising briefly against the light on the horizon, it showed the rounded, lobed snout—the "cow nose" from which its name derives. A slender tail snaked out from its rear.

Chesapeake rays winter off the coast of Venezuela, timing their migration so as to arrive in these parts early in June. Their mating dances, in which they skitter together over the water like skipping stones, are rarely seen. By September they will have started to move southward again.

JUNE 18

Kent Island

Shoreline development has reduced or eliminated nesting habitat for many of the birds of the Chesapeake. The delicate and environmentally sensitive least tern, which once bred on sandy beaches throughout the Bay area, has suffered the most drastic decline. Of their more than fifty historically known breeding colonies, only three remain, on isolated islands in the lower Bay.

Within the past decade, the terns have shown a surprising, if not desperate, adaptation. They have managed to nest successfully on the flat roofs of large buildings. The slag and pebble surfaces closely resemble conditions the birds once found on sandy beaches. Moreover, they are free from most predators and from the dangers of flooding.

Least terns have nested on the roofs of high schools and they have used the flat tops of car dealerships and shopping centers. Somehow they have found safety and security above the hubbub of human activity just below them. Such adaptation has surely saved the least tern from extirpation on the Chesapeake.

As I approached one of these terneries today, situated atop a busy shopping center, the sky was alive with their slim, graceful forms. Creatures too delicate and lovely, they seemed, for such vulgar surroundings. Several times paired birds spiraled upward, facing each other, then fluttered and hovered together, chattering excitedly. Others carried small fish dangling from their yellow bills, which they had caught in nearby Thompson Creek.

We were there to erect a temporary wire fence to prevent the young terns from falling off or becoming imprisoned in the storm gutters. During past summers, many had fallen into these drains and, too weak to escape, were eventually washed to the ground, where they fell prey to dogs, cats, and careless humans.

The project offered an opportunity to study the young terns at close range. Those just out of the egg were largely white, with touches of mouse gray mottling on the head and back. Ternlets a bit older showed tinges of

pale ochre with darker markings. Too weak to stand, they still crouched in the nest scrape. Older, larger chicks were quite mobile, running swiftly to the only cover available, the overhang of an air conditioner. Here, and in other corners of the roof, they crowded in groups of eight to ten birds, forming a sort of crèche. Much rust showed in their juvenal plumage, with dark tips marbling the feathers.

These patterns, intended by nature to match the color and texture of sandy beaches, closely resembled the roofing material. So well camouflaged were the youngest chicks, that one had to be careful not to step on them.

Two other roof-born chicks, baby killdeers, were even better concealed. Their gray and white natal down, with dark accents, precisely matched the roofing gravel. These little shorebirds showed no fear, drowsing sleepily with eyes half-closed, their oversized, pinkish gray legs folded beneath them.

Their parents raised quite a ruckus when I came near. One limped pitiably, dragging its wing as if broken, while its mate flew above, shrieking.

Bloodsworth Island

The map of southern Dorchester County shows an intricate tracery of scrolled and curled waterways. Winding, intertwining creeks snake through a jigsaw puzzle of islands and narrow peninsulas. But the chart is accurate only when the tide is low; at flood tide, much of what shows as land becomes water. That was how it looked this mist-heavy morning as spring turned toward summer.

Paved roads were bridges, connecting pine-clad hummocks and ridges of high ground where houses and sheds clustered. Roadside ditches were brimming with an incoming tide that, having overflowed the marshes, covered the roadway as well.

Much of the mapped shoreline had become one with the Bay. Side trails of sand and oystershell meandered off into the marsh, whole sections of them disappearing beneath the water, then rising again.

One such elevated segment provided a suitable nesting site for diamondback terrapins. Two of them were crawling atop a sandy tump, where another had begun to lay her eggs. Less than half of her carapace showed above the burrow she had dug and backed into. Her front legs groped weakly in midair under the strain of dropping her eggs. Her pearly gray head and legs were delicately scrawled and spotted. Another, with a darker,

almost unmarked head, was looking for a suitably soft spot. She tested the ground first with her front feet and, finding it too hard, moved on. A few yards farther, she tried again and, encouraged, began to dig with her back legs. The effort lifted her several inches off the ground. She soon tired here as well and gave up, leaving in the sand a small hole and an imprint of her body.

The tide had flushed a family of clapper rails into the open. The mother rail led her newly hatched brood of chicks over floating debris and even into deep water. Though they were only tiny bits of black fluff, they managed to keep afloat. Another adult rail swam across a nearby gut,

nervous and fidgety at being in the open. And a bit farther on, one more young rail, older and larger but still in juvenile black, was foraging on its own. A gangly young willet caught in the open ran for cover.

When the fog gave way to the morning sun, the warmth brought to the surface dozens of terrapins, only their heads appearing above the gentle swell. The mouth of the creek was peppered with them.

From a distance, the dominant feature of Bloodsworth, the largest in a group of islands a mile offshore, was a series of three-tiered platforms erected on telephone poles. Each supported the bulky nest of a great blue heron. Adult herons and full-grown

juveniles stood guard nearby. A grove of spindly pines supported a few nests, and still more were clumped in a grove of red cedar.

The fallen remnants of a pine forest littered the marsh along Fin Creek, a narrow stream that nearly bisects the island. This decimation is said to have resulted from an accidental spraying of napalm. Or was it a casualty of practice bombing? Gaping holes in the marsh and huge craters in flats were certainly the result of such impacts. The military has long used these islands for target practice.

Yet the place seemed untouched, primeval. From the head of Fin Creek, deep within the prairielike expanse, one confronted a world of two immensities: a vault of sky above an endless vista of marsh. The smooth, undulating sweep of greening cordgrass was broken only by stands of gray brown needle rush. A harrier, skimming over this expanse, seemed Lilliputian in the vastness. The rich cinnamon underparts of a female glinted in the sun. She followed a level course until suddenly the white of her rump flashed and she swerved toward her blue gray mate, who had approached unnoticed. He carried prey of some sort tucked under his tail.

As their paths crossed, he lowered his legs, revealing the duckling he carried. With the flick of a wing, his mate pirouetted lightly, reached up and snatched it. Did she catch it in midair, after it was dropped? Or take it directly from his grasp? In any case, the exchange cleanly made, they both continued on without pause, fading from view beyond a growth of low cedars.

Passing Pone Island, we reached Adam Island, where a crescent of beach curled inside an inlet. Within the opening a succession of wet mudflats mingled opalescent browns and grays where pools of shimmering blue water reflected a gathering of gulls and terns.

On the berm of the beach here were strewn the broken remains of terrapin eggs. The bits of shell were pliant and stringy. Was this a nest unearthed by a predator or the remains of a successfully hatched clutch?

Holland Island, the farthest from the mainland, was once a thriving community with a school and a ballpark. It has eroded into three fragments, only one house still clinging to the smallest segment. On the largest, two wooded tracts persist, mostly of Virginia pine and persimmon. In its center, tidal pools gleamed in an open meadow of salt marsh. A pair of noisy willets declared their ownership of this bit of real estate, which they shared with a family of gadwall busily tipping in the shallows.

A mixed colony of snowy egrets, tricolored herons, and little blue herons were nesting in a thick grove of persimmon trees. An understory of bayberry and marsh elder provided dense cover, concealing most of the nests. Higher nests were in the open. In one exposed bulk of sticks stood two young snowies, almost ready to fledge. In their anxiety (or curiosity) they nearly fell from their flimsy shelter. Balancing on a branch nearby, two young tricolored herons glared, their heads fuzzy and frazzled with down. Despite such comic dishabille, there was elegance in their maroon necks, smartly striped with white.

Great egrets nested here, too, the returning adults floating buoyantly overhead, legs dangling. A cluster of great blue heron nests was crammed into a single dead pine. Full-grown young crowded some nests; others held chicks still in downy white.

JUNE 20

Spring Island

Tiny, treeless Spring Island maintains an uncertain, perilous existence midway in the Holland Straits, between the larger masses of Bloodsworth and South Marsh Islands. Somehow this scrap of marshland has withstood the buffeting of wave and wind that has washed away many more substantial corners of the Chesapeake. One storm could wipe it off the map.

Yet nesting gulls find it a haven, an isle undisturbed, free from predation, far from the human traffic that everywhere plagues those birds that live on beaches. White flecks against the green grasses, the gulls showed little concern as our small boat neared shore. Quite suspicious, however, were the half dozen oystercatchers that rushed out to greet us with raucous complaint. Clownish in appearance, with oversized scarlet bills, pink feet, and bold black and white plumage, they were nevertheless quite serious in their intent. They mobbed us as fearlessly as they would a passing hawk.

When we remained on direct course for their island home, their frenzy increased. And then the gulls finally joined in dissent, lifting in one dense, clamoring pack. Mostly herring gulls, with the sun full upon them, there was startling beauty in the dazzling white of several hundred birds rising against the deep blue of the sky. There was also bedlam, their combined protestations increasing to a bawling roar. Scattered among them were a dozen or so great black-backed gulls, their baritone barking punctuating the clamor. A lone common tern, slim and delicate, flew above the furor, adding its own cries of alarm.

A smaller contingent of laughing gulls, resplendent with jet black hoods, dove gray upperparts, and creamy breasts, kept to the opposite shore of a nearby inlet. Rather than take noisily to wing, they remained on the water, watching with a nervous intensity. They had nested in the spartina meadows beyond the tall grasses at the stream's edge.

Coarse stands of needle rush covered parts of the island, its perpetual purplish brown contrasting with the bright green spartina. Much of the vegetation was a pale yellow green, matted and trampled by hundreds of webbed feet. Here the herring gulls had fashioned their nests, simple circular platforms of woven grass.

Most of the nests were empty, but nearby many of the fledglings, balls of grayish fluff, crouched under tufts of grass. The older and larger birds were quite mobile and ran to seek better cover. In one nest huddled two chicks,

the smaller having just hatched. Its natal down was still wet and matted. The bill was gray with a pink tip, the "egg tooth" used to break through the shell. Too weak to lift its head, it panted in the afternoon heat. Its sibling, possibly a week older, was alert and strong. Well feathered, its buff colored back was peppered with black. One youngster had fallen into the water, and though it could swim strongly, was struggling to get back up on land. A timely wave gave it the necessary lift.

Three nests contained a single egg. Brownish ochre, scrawled with chocolate, each was about the size of a chicken's egg. Possibly they were infertile. The corpses of two chicks were decaying amid fish bones and other marine detritus.

The squalling of the gulls rose and fell in intensity as we walked the shore. Willets hung above the grasses, giving vent to their own outrage. All the while the oystercatchers continued to shout derision.

Lying motionless on a strip of beach, huddled next to a bundle of driftweed, was the source of their concern. A young oystercatcher, its bill and head pressed close to the earth, was partly hidden under a bit of wrack. The ruddy color of its underparts, barred and mottled with dark brown, closely matched the color of the sand, and the youngster had instinctively trusted its natural camouflage. One of its parents, in desperation, feigned an injured wing to draw attention away from the chick.

The noisy pair continued to pour invective until we pushed off. As they had come to greet us, so they bade us farewell. The gulls, desperate to return to nests and young, were alighting as we left.

JUNE 21

Beverly Beach County Park

In predawn darkness, a heavy surf rolled across the narrow strand of beach, slopping over the bulkhead. The month's highest tide was further driven by a strong nor'easter, creating conditions hardly amenable for the horseshoe crabs to come ashore, mate, and lay eggs. Could they even approach the shore under such buffeting?

But come they did. With the first stain of red on the horizon, we could see them, gathered beyond the bulkhead where a shelf of sand was exposed. Others were struggling just offshore on a narrow strip of wave-washed beach. And farther down the beach, the backs of still others reflected the low, slanting light.

In the Chesapeake region, horseshoe crabs come ashore during May and June to mate and lay eggs. Following ancient rhythms, their spawning is coordinated with the full moon and evening spring tides. And they need undisturbed sandy beaches, where the females can scoop out shallow nests and deposit their eggs.

First come the males, followed a week or two later by the larger females. To attract a mate, the female releases a chemical substance called a pheromone, which serves as a sexual stimulant. The male, using special claspers on the tips of his forelegs, hooks onto the female as she approaches the beach. She then leads him to the water's edge, digs out a nest, and deposits the eggs, which are fertilized as she drags him over them.

But how could they possibly mate today, with such wind and waves? How could they bury their eggs with most of the narrow beach underwater? And even then, could they be fertilized? As the females burrowed into the sand, the waves washed over and around them, filling the cavities as they were dug and tumbling over many of the crabs. Most of those that were upturned soon managed to right themselves, bracing with the stiff tail (the telson). But many remained helplessly on their backs.

The females managed somehow to pull, or rather drag, the grasping males. Most of the females were attended by several males, though only one, attached to her abdomen, could effectively fertilize the eggs. The others encircled her, carapaces touching. One group formed a star, in perfect symmetry, the female in the center.

As the sky brightened, most of the females began easing back into deep water, the males still clinging. But others continued to dig nests, pushing up

ridges of sand before them. Many of the round, opaque greenish eggs, smaller than BB shot, washed along the tideline.

Birds crowded in to feed on the eggs. Grackles and starlings searched among the tidal detritus, as did a lone song sparrow. Tiny craters, rimmed with sand, marked where the birds had found and excavated nests. Other creatures, most likely raccoons, had also feasted on the bounty. Two large dead female horseshoes had been attacked, their underbodies gnawed, their eggs strewn about.

If they survive predation, the eggs mature and hatch in the two weeks between this spring tide (the high tide that occurs with the new and the full moon) and the neap tide (the low tide that comes with the moon's first and third quarters). After hatching, the baby horseshoes dig out of the sand and make their way back to the water. Unlike most marine invertebrates, which pass through several immature stages, they begin life as miniature adults.

The whitened skeletons of these newborn horseshoes littered the dry sand. Barely one-half inch across (some were even smaller), they were replicas of the adults, with shells and appendages still intact. But where did they come from? Were these hatchlings from the previous high tide? Had they never made their way to deep water? Or were they washed back from the sea?

We counted 225 adult crabs in about one hundred yards of exposed sand, too narrow to be properly called a beach. Though this was not an impressive count when compared to the millions that throng to Delaware Bay and to much wider coastal beaches, these primitive creatures served as a reminder of an ancient rite of spring, one that had its origins long before there were dinosaurs. Long, long before.

PLACE NAMES

Maryland

Barren Island, Dorchester Co.

Beverly Beach County Park, Anne
    Arundel Co.

Black Swamp Creek, Prince Georges Co.

Bloodsworth Island, Dorchester Co.

Bodkin Island, Queen Annes Co.

Cheston Creek, Anne Arundel Co.

Choptank River at Dover Bridge, Talbot Co.

Deal Island, Somerset Co.

Deep Creek, Anne Arundel Co.

Eastern Neck Island, Kent Co.

Flag Ponds County Park, Calvert Co.

Glebe Creek, Anne Arundel Co.

Hill's Bridge, Anne Arundel Co.

Jug Bay Wetlands Center, Anne Arundel Co.

Kent Island, Queen Annes Co.

Kings Landing County Park, Calvert Co.

Lyons Creek, between Anne Arundel and
    Calvert Co.

Marumsco Creek, Somerset Co.

Mayo Beach, Anne Arundel Co.

Merkle Wildlife Management Area,
    Prince Georges Co.

Muddy Creek, Anne Arundel Co.

Nanticoke River, Wicomico and
    Dorchester Co.

Nassawango Creek, Worcester Co.

Otter Point Estuarine Sanctuary,
    Harford Co.

Patuxent River Park, Prince Georges Co.

Pennington Pond, Anne Arundel Co.

Popham Creek, Anne Arundel Co.

Poplar Island, Talbot Co.

Rhode River, Anne Arundel Co.

Sellman Creek, Anne Arundel Co.

Sheepshead Cove, off Sellman Creek,
    Anne Arundel Co.

Shoreham Beach, Anne Arundel Co.

South River, Anne Arundel Co.

Spring Island, Dorchester Co.

Susquehanna State Park, Harford Co.

Taylor's Island, Dorchester Co.

Thomas Point, Anne Arundel Co.

Triton Beach, Anne Arundel Co.

Tuckahoe Creek, Queen Annes and
    Caroline Co.

Turkey Point, Anne Arundel Co.

West River, Anne Arundel Co.

Wye Island, Queen Anne's Co.

Virginia

Corrotoman River, Northumberland Co.

Dragon Run, Middlesex Co.

Wakefield, Westmoreland Co.

SCIENTIFIC NAMES

Alewife—*Alosa pseudoharengus*

American Crow—*Corvus brachyrhynchos*

American Goldeneye—*Bucephala clangula*

American Holly—*Ilex opaca*

American Oystercatcher—*Haemotopus bachmani*

American Robin—*Turdus migratorius*

American Shad—*Alosa sapidissima*

American Wigeon—*Anas americana*

American Woodcock—*Scolopax minor*

Arrow Arum—*Peltandra virginica*

Ash Tree—*Fraxinus pensylvanica*

Atlantic Menhaden—*Brevoortia tyrannus*

Bald Cypress—*Taxodium distichum*

Bald Eagle—*Haliaetus albicola*

Barn Swallow—*Hirundo rustica*

Barred Owl—*Strix varia*

Bayberry—*Myrica pensylvanica*

Bay-breasted Warbler—*Dendroica castenea*

Beech—*Fagus grandiflolia*

Big Cordgrass—*Spartinia cynosuroides*

Black and White Warbler—*Mniotilta varia*

Black-backed Gull—*Larus marinus*

Black-bellied Plover—*Pluvialis squatrola*

Blackburnian Warbler—*Dendroica fusca*

Black Crappie—*Pomoxis nigromaculatus*

Black Duck—*Anas rubripes*

Black Haw—*Viburnum prunifolium*

Black Walnut Tree—*Juglans nigra*

Black Willow—*Salix nigra*

Bloodroot—*Sanguinaria canadensis*

Blueback Herring—*Alosa aestivalis*

Bluebird—*Sialia sialis*

Blue Flag—*Iris versicolor*

Bonaparte's Gull—*Larus philadelphia*

Brown Thrasher—*Toxostoma rufum*

Bufflehead—*Bucephala albeola*

Bullfrog—*Rana catesbiana*

Canada Goose—*Branta canadensis*

Canada Warbler—*Wilsonia canadensis*

Canvasback—*Athya valisineria*

Carolina Chickadee—*Parus carolinensis*

Carolina Willow—*Salix caroliniana*

Carolina Wren—*Thryothorus ludovicianus*

Carp—*Cyprinus carpio*

Caspian Tern—*Sterna caspia*

Cattail—*Typha latifolia*

Cattle Egret—*Bubulcus ibis*

Channel Catfish—*Ictalurus punctatus*

Cherry Tree (Bird Cherry)—*Prunus avium*

Chickweed—*Stellaria media*

Chokeberry—*Aronia arbutifolia*

Chorus Frog—*Pseudacris triseriata*

Clapper Rail—*Rallus longirostris*

Common Carp—*Cyprinus carpio*

Common Goldeneye—*Bucephala clangula*

Common Grackle—*Quiscalus quiscula*

Common Loon—*Gavia immer*

Common Snipe—*Gallinago gallinago*

Common Tern—*Sterna hirundo*

Cottontail Rabbit—*Sylvilagus floridanus*

Cownose Ray—*Rhinoptera quadriloba*

Crow—*Corvus brachyrhynchos*

Diamondback Terrapin—*Malaclemys terrapin*

Double-crested Cormorant—*Phalacrocorax auritus*

Dreamy Dusky-wing—*Erynnis icelus*

Dunlin—*Calidris alpina*

Dutchman's Breeches—*Dicentra cucullaria*

Eastern Bluebird—*Sialia sialia*

Elderberry—*Sambucus canadensis*

Falcate Orange-tip—*Falcapica midea*

Fiddler Crab—*Uca spp.*

Field Pansy—*Viola rafinesquei*

Flycatcher—*Tyrannidae spp.*

Forster's Tern—*Sterna forsteri*

Gadwall—*Anas strepera*

Gray Treefrog—*Hyla versicolor*

Great Blue Heron—*Ardea herodias*

Great Egret—*Casmerodius albus*

Great Horned Owl—*Bubo virginianus*

Great Spangled Fritillary—*Speyeria cybele*

Greater Scaup—*Aythya marila*

Greater Yellowlegs—*Tringa melanoleuca*

Green-backed Heron—*Butorides striatus*

Green-winged Teal—*Anas crecca*

Groundsel Tree—*Baccharis halimifolia*

Hermit Thrush—*Catharus guttatus*

Herring Gull—*Larus argentatus*

Honeysuckle—*Lonicera japonica*

Hooded Warbler—*Wilsonia citrina*

Horned Grebe—*Podiceps auritus*

Horned Pondweed—*Zannichellia palustris*

Horseshoe Crab—*Limulus polyphemus*

Horsetail—*Equisetum arvense*

Interrupted Fern—*Osmunda claytonia*

Killdeer—*Charadrius vociferus*

Kingfisher—*Megaceryle alcyon*

Laughing Gull—*Larus atricilla*

Least Tern—*Sterna antillarum*

Little Blue Heron—*Egretta caerula*

Loblolly Pine—*Pinus taeda*

Longnose Gar—*Lepisosteus osseus*

Loon—*Gavia immer*

Magnolia Warbler—*Dendroica magnolia*

Maple—*Acer rubrum*

Marsh Elder—*Iva frutescens*

Mayapple—*Podophyllum peltatum*

Mockingbird—*Mimus polyglottos*

Morel—*Morchella spp.*

Mourning Cloak—*Nymphalis antiopia*

Mud Turtle—*Kinosternon subrubrum*

Muskrat—*Ondatra zibethicus*

Needle Rush—*Juncas roemerianus*

Nightingale—*Luscinia megarhyncos*

Northern Flicker-*Colaptes auratus*

Northern Gannet—*Sula bassanus*

Northern Harrier—*Circus cyaneus*

Northern Pintail—*Anas acuta*

Northern Rough-winged Swallow—*Steligidopteryx serrripennis*

Oak—*Quercus spp.*

Old Squaw—*Clangula hyemalis*

Orchard Oriole—*Icterus spurius*

Osprey—*Pandion haliaetus*

Ovenbird—*Sierus aurocapillus*

Painted Turtle—*Chrysemys picta*

Palm Warbler—*Dendroica palmarum*

Parula Warbler—*Parula americana*

Pearl Crescent—*Phycoides tharos*

Persimmon—*Diospryos virginiana*

Pickerelweed—*Pontederia cordata*

Pink Azalea—*Rhododendron nudiflorum*

Pine Warbler—*Dendroica pinus*

Polyporus—*Polyporus versicolor*

Prothonotary Warbler—*Protonotaria citrea*

Puffball—*Lycoperdon spp.*

Purple Martin—*Progne subis*

Red Bay—*Persea Borbonia*

Red-breasted Merganser—*Mergus serrator*

Redbud—*Cersis canadensis*

Red Cedar—*Juniperus virginiana*

Red-eyed Vireo—*Vireo olivaceus*

Red Fox—*Vulpes vulpes*

Red Maples—*Acer rubrum*

Red-shouldered Hawk—*Buteo lineatus*

Redstart—*Setophaga ruticilla*

Red-winged Blackbird—*Agelaius phoeniceus*

Ring-billed Gull—*Larus delawarensis*

River Birch—*Betula nigra*

River Otter—*Lutra canadensis*

Robin—*Turdus migratorius*

Rose-breasted Grosbeak—*Pheucticus ludovicianus*

Rose Mallow—*Hibiscus moscheutos*

Ruby-crowned Kinglet—*Regulus calendula*

Ruddy Duck—*Oxyura jamaicensis*

Salt Marsh Grass—*Spartina alterniflora*

Savannah Sparrow—*Passerculus sandwichensis*

Scarlet Tanager—*Piranga olivacea*

Sea Rocket—*Cakile edentula*

Shad—*Alosa sapidissima*

Shadbush—*Amelanchier spp.*

Sharp-shinned Hawk—*Accipiter velox*

Silver-spotted Skipper—*Epargyreus clarus*

Smooth Alder—*Alnus serrulata*

Smooth Arrowwood—*Viburnum recognitum*

Snapping Turtle—*Chelydra serpentina*

Snowy Egret—*Egretta thula*

Song Sparrow—*Melospiza melodia*

Spatterdock, Pond-lily—*Nymphaea advena*

Speedwell—*Veronica persica*

Spicebush—*Benzoin aestivale*

Spotted Salamander—*Ambystoma maculatum*

Spotted Sandpiper—*Actitis macularia*

Spring Azure—*Celastrina ladon*

Spring Beauty—*Claytonia virginica*

Spring Peeper—*Hyla crucifer*

Starling—*Stumus vulgaris*

Stork's-bill—*Erodium cicutarium*

Striped Bass—*Morone saxatilis*

Swamp Milkweed—*Asclepias incarnata*

Sweet Bay—*Magnolia virginiana*

Sweet Flag—*Calamus acorus*

Sweet Gum Tree—*Liquidambar styraciflua*

Sycamore—*Platanus occidentalis*

Tassel-white—*Itea virginica*

Three-square—*Scirpus spp.*

Tiger swallowtail—*Pterousus glaucus*

Tree Swallow—*Tachycineta bicolor*

Tricolored Heron—*Egretta tricolor*

Tulip Poplar—*Liriodendron tulipifera*

Tundra Swan—*Cygnus columbianus*

Virginia Pine—*Pinus virginiana*

Weeping Willow—*Salix babylonica*

Whippoorwill—*Caprimulgus vociferus*

White Catfish—*Ameiurus catus*

White Perch—*Morone americana*

White-eyed Vireo—*Vireo griseus*

White-throated Sparrow—*Zonotrichia albicollis*

Wild Rice—*Zizania aquatica*

Willet—*Catoptrophorus semipalmatus*

Winterberry Holly—*Ilex verticillata*

Woodchuck—*Marmota monax*

Wood Frog—*Rana sylvatica*

Wood Duck—*Aix sponsa*

Yellow-bellied Sapsucker—*Sphyrapicus varius*

Yellow Morel—*Morchella esculenta*

Yellow Mustard—*Brassica spp.*

Yellow Perch—*Perca flavescens*

Yellow Pond Lily—*Nuphar advena*

Yellow-rumped Warbler—*Dendroica coronata*

Yellowthroat Warbler-*Dendroica dominica*